New River Gorge Trail Guide

Second Edition

Hiking and Biking Trails of the New River Gorge National River, Cranberry Wilderness Area and the Greenbrier River Trail.

By
Steve Cater

New River Gorge Trail Guide
Hiking and Biking Trails of the New River Gorge National River,
Cranberry Glades and Greenbrier River Trail.
First Edition 1996
Second Edition Copyright © 2000 by Steve Cater

ISBN 0-9678270-2-7

King Coal Propaganda
PO Box 471
Fayetteville, WV 25840
http://NewRiverGorge.net

Cover: View of the New River Gorge from the Endless Wall Trail. Photo: Steve Cater

Table of Contents ————————

View of the famous New River Gorge Bridge from Long Point.

A section of Sandstone Falls on the upper New River.

· Introduction ·

Hiking and biking are fun for everyone. These activities appeal to all that have a love for the outdoors and a zest for adventure. The vast mountainous areas of West Virginia offer an opportunity of exploration for the experienced and novice hiker and biker. Breathtaking vistas of rugged mountain terrain, abundant wildlife and a healthy appetite for adventure together form the ultimate nature experience.

This is the first published guidebook to focus entirely on the New River Gorge Area, Cranberry Glades and the Greenbrier Trail. This book includes the numerous trails of the New River Gorge River, Babcock State Park, Hawk's Nest State Park, Cranberry Wilderness Area and the Greenbrier River Trail. The result is a collection of enjoyable trails for the outdoor enthusiast to explore.

A quick overview of the areas in this book will reveal that trails in the New River Gorge, Babcock State Park, and Hawk's Nest tend to be short day hikes varying from one quarter mile to eight miles in length. The Cranberry Area offers a true wilderness experience where it is possible to backpack for several days in an isolated setting. The Greenbrier Trail offers multiple day mountain biking and backpacking as well as short day hikes. These areas were selected due to their uniqueness and close proximity to each other. Each area is unique in its own way and visitors using this book will be able to easily select trails and plan trips according to their abilities and agenda.

Warning

User Beware! The author, publisher and distributors of this book are not responsible for inaccurate information, condition of trails, absence of trails, savage dogs, gnarly mountain people, twisted ankles, and any other ill begotten woes that fate bestows upon users of this book. Assume responsibility for your own actions, be careful and enjoy yourself!

Location

The areas described in this book are all located in southern West Virginia. This region lies within the Appalachian Mountains and is characterized as rugged terrain with steep hills and deep river gorges. Forests are mainly deciduous with many conifers at higher elevations. The elevation varies from about 1100 feet in the New River Gorge to 4600 feet in the Cranberry Area. The areas featured in this book are all within 1.5 hours drive of each other.

Climate

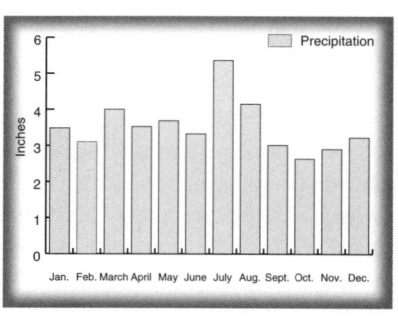

The climate in West Virginia changes dramatically with the seasons. Summer (mid-June to mid-Sept.) tends to be hot and humid with temperatures ranging from the 70's to upper 80's during the day and 60's to 70's at night. It is common to have 70% to 80% humidity during the summer. Winter temperatures range from the 20's to 50's with the occasional drop to sub zero temperatures. The spring and fall seasons have the mildest weather and are perhaps the most beautiful time of the year. Fall (mid-Sept. to Nov. 1) is generally dry with temperatures in the 50's to 70's and low humidity. Spring temperatures also vary from the 60's to 70's. The higher elevations are generally 5 to 10 degrees cooler. Precipitation for the year averages around 60 inches. The Cranberry Area usually has cooler temperatures and receives a large amount of snowfall during the winter months making it an excellent cross-country skiing area.

Hazards

Luckily the area is relatively free from man eating predators. There are black bears in the Cranberry area but they are very timid and avoid humans. However, proper food storage is highly recommended. Poisonous snakes such as the copperhead and rattlesnake are fairly common so be careful and mindful of where you sit and place your hands. Mosquitos, black flies and deer fly are the main insect culprits that may cause the most irritation but insect repellant will keep them at bay. Be aware of poison ivy and know how to identify the shiny three leaf plant that grows on a vine. This easy to spot plant could make the difference between a great experience and a miserable experience.

Trails and Equipment

The trails described in this book are mainly National Park Service, State Park and National Forest Service trails. Many of the trails are old logging roads or old railroad beds. These old roads have a gradual gradient and range from 4 feet to 8 feet in width. The area was extensively logged and mined in the past and the remains of these roads crisscross the steep hills. Trails are designated as hiking trails and/or biking trails. This designation is determined by the organization that administers the park. In some places mountain bikes are not allowed on trails where extensive erosion occurs or where there is a high amount of foot traffic. An exception to this is the Cranberry Wilderness Area where vehicles and bikes are prohibited. If you disagree with the designation of trails write the agency that administers the area.

Do not drink water from streams or rivers unless it has been filtered with a proper filtering device.

When hiking or biking in any of the areas described, always wear suitable clothing and bring sufficient water, food, first aid kit and bike tools. Be familiar with basic first aid and the symptoms of hypothermia. During the spring and fall seasons, temperatures and weather may vary dramatically, especially at higher elevations. Be prepared for the worst! Wear adequate clothing and footgear. It is better to be overdressed than underdressed. Taking off layers that you don't need is nicer than having to put on layers that you don't have! For most trails, light to medium hiking boots are appropriate. Avoid cotton clothing in wet and cold conditions.

Map Symbols

Below is a key for map symbols used throughout this book. Distances stated in trail descriptions are one-way (OW) or roundtrip (RT). Areas are shown from bird's-eye view perspectives or from profiles and in many cases a profile and top view are shown for each area. The profile maps give an excellent perspective on the verticle relief of the area but keep in mind some verticle exaggeration occurs. The maps were designed using USGS information but inaccuraccies do occur. If you are in need of highly accurate information use the USGS 7.5 minute quads. Trail conditions and locations may change due to natural forces or man-made changes so be mindful of this fact while out on the trail.

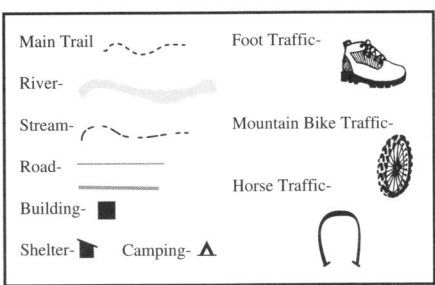

Main Trail-
River-
Stream-
Road-
Building-
Shelter-   Camping- ▲
Foot Traffic-
Mountain Bike Traffic-
Horse Traffic-

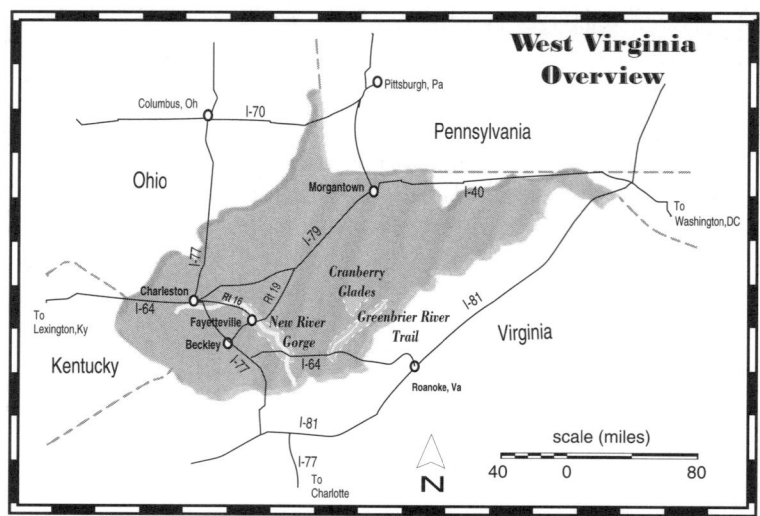

West Virginia Overview

Columbus, Oh

I-70

Pittsburgh, Pa

Pennsylvania

Ohio

Morgantown

I-40

I-79

To Washington,DC

Cranberry Glades

Charleston

Rt 16

Rt 19

I-77

I-64

To Lexington,Ky

Fayetteville

New River Gorge

Greenbrier River Trail

I-81

Virginia

Beckley

I-64

Kentucky

I-77

Roanoke, Va

I-81

I-77

To Charlotte

scale (miles)

40   0   80

N

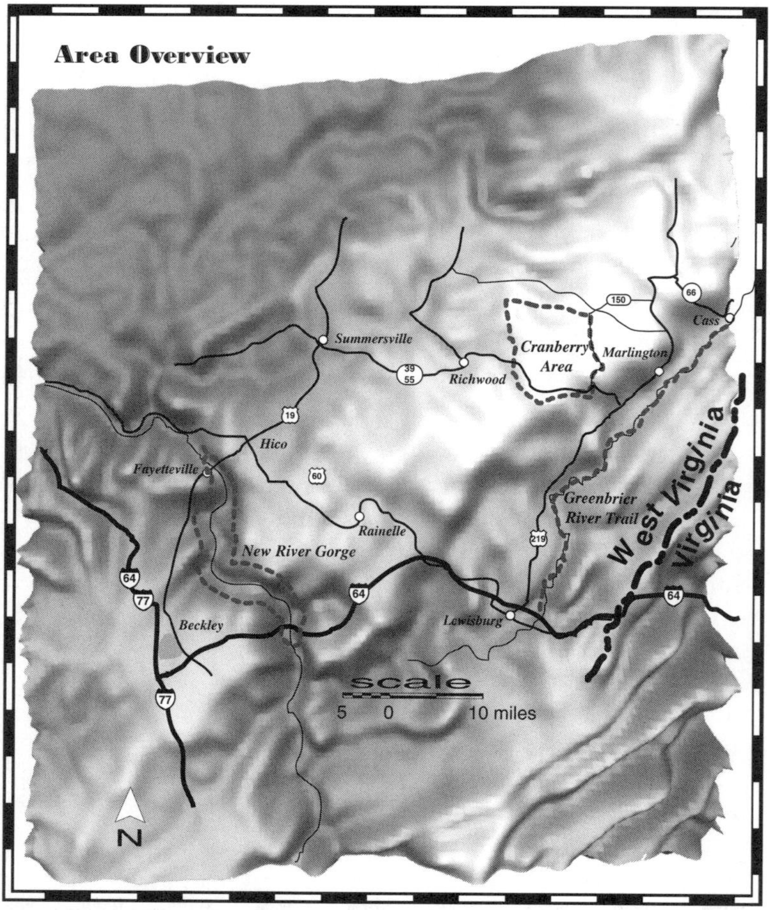

Area Overview

Summersville

150

66

Cass

Cranberry Area

Marlington

39 55

Richwood

15

Hico

60

Greenbrier River Trail

West Virginia

Virginia

Fayetteville

Rainelle

New River Gorge

219

64

64

64

Beckley

Lewisburg

77

scale

5   0   10 miles

N

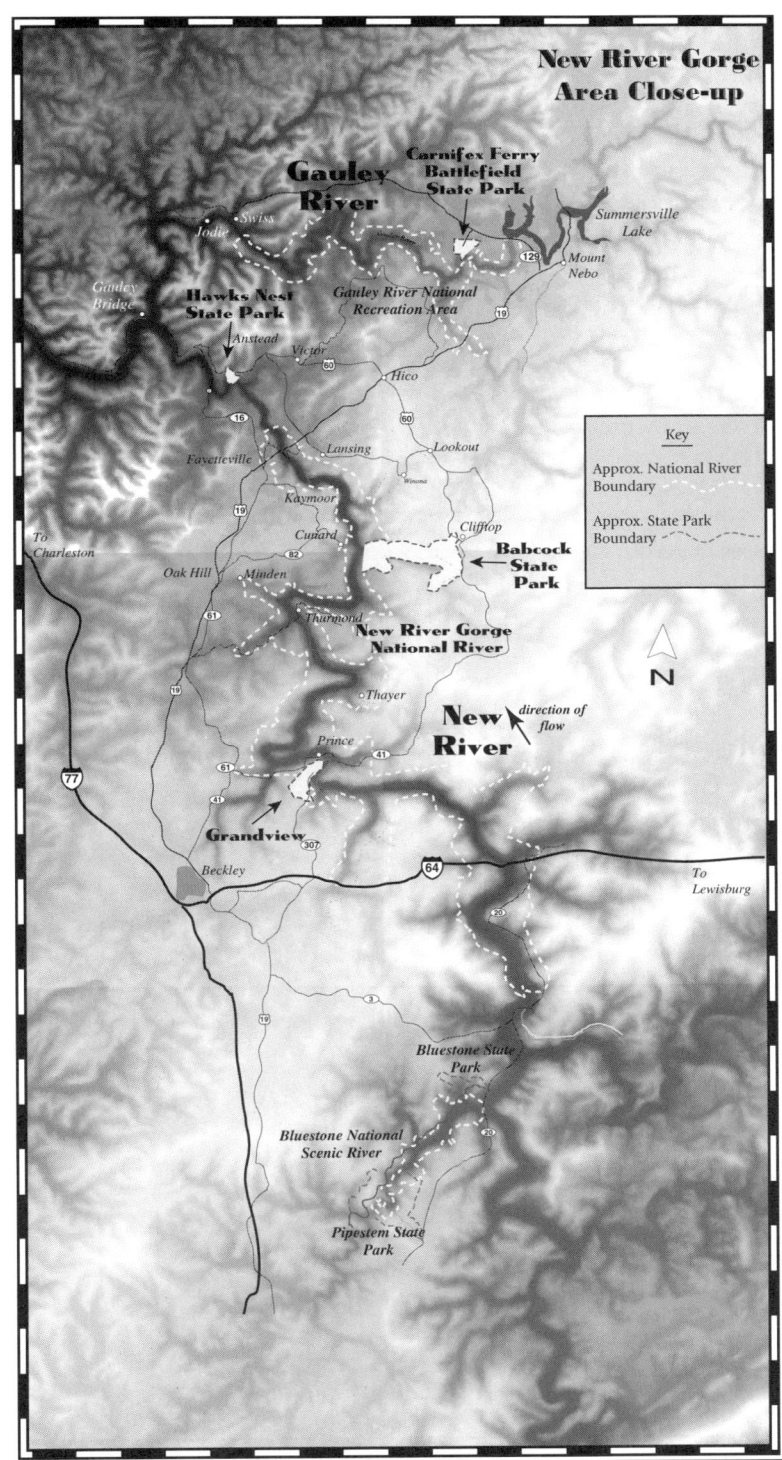

**New River Gorge
Area Close-up**

Carnifex Ferry
Battlefield
State Park

**Gauley
River**

Jodie
Swiss
Summersville
Lake

129

Mount
Nebo

*Gauley
Bridge*

19

**Hawks Nest
State Park**

*Gauley River National
Recreation Area*

Anstead

Victor

Hico

60

16

60

Lansing
Lookout

Fayetteville
Woona

Key

19

Kaymoor

Approx. National River
Boundary

Cunard
Clifftop

82

**Babcock
State
Park**

*To
Charleston*

Oak Hill
Minden

**New River Gorge
National River**

61

Thurmond

19

N

Thayer

77

Prince

41

**New
River**

*direction of
flow*

61

41

Grandview
307

Beckley

64

*To
Lewisburg*

20

19

3

**Bluestone State
Park**

**Bluestone National
Scenic River**

20

**Pipestem State
Park**

Environmental Concerns

Be kind to the environment, it is already under a great deal of strain. As Americans, our presence creates far more environmental damage than we realize. Most of our lives revolve around petroleum powered automobiles, coal generated power, and man-made chemicals. All of these products, in one way or another, do a great deal of damage to the natural environment. We consume much of the worlds resources not out of necessity, but in trivial often wasteful pursuits. Attempt to lessen your impact on the natural world by living simply. While hiking, biking, rafting, sight-seeing, etc.., try and observe these simple rules:

> • *Do not destroy any types of vegetation.*
> • *Use dead wood for firewood. Never chop down a living tree. Use only established fire pits or better yet use camp stoves.*
> • *Pack-out and pickup trash and cigarette butts.*
> • *Bury human waste and toilet paper at least 6 inches and never near water.*
> • *Stay on trails and avoid short cuts. This reduces erosion.*
> • *Relax and enjoy the outdoors and don't fall prey to the uptight white guy syndrome.*

Outdoor Activities

Rafting- The New and Gauley Rivers are two of the best commercial whitewater rivers in the country. There are approximately 20 commercial outfitters in the area who run the river. The rafting season usually starts around mid-April and finish in late October. The annual dam release of the Gauley River is one of the high points of the season. The Gauley is one of the most intense commercial runs in the country and the fall season is one of the busiest times of the year for the rafting outfitters. Below is a list of local rafting guide services listed in alphabetical order. All of these outfits are professional organizations but prices vary.

ACE Whitewater- 1-800-787-3982 or (304) 469-2651.
Adventures- 1-800- 879-7483 or (304) 574-3834.
Appalachian Wildwater- 1-800- 624-8060.
Class VI- 1-800-252-7784 or (304) 574-0704.
Drift-A-Bit- 1-800-633-RAFT or (304) 574-3282.
Mountain River Tours- 1-800-822-1386 or (304) 658-5266.
New and Gauley River Expeditions- 1-800-472-7238.
New and Gauley River Adventures- 1-800-SKY-RAFT or (304) 574-3008.
New River Scenic Whitewater Tours- 1-800-282-0880 or (304) 466-2288.
North American River Runners- 1-800-950-2585.
Passages to Adventure- 1-800-634-3785.
The Rivermen- 1-800-545-7238 or (304) 574-0515.
Rivers Whitewater Rafting- 1-800-879-7483 or (304) 574-3824.
Songer Whitewater- 1-800-356-RAFT or (304) 658-9926.

USA Raft- 1-800-346-RAFT or (304) 574-3655.
West Virginia Whitewater- (304) 574-0871.
Whitewater Information- 1-800-782-RAFT or (304) 574-1003.
Wildwater Expeditions- 1-800-WVA-RAFT or (304) 658-4008.

Kayaking- The New River, Gauley River and Meadow River are extremely popular with kayakers. These three rivers plus numerous smaller drainages provide kayakers with a variety of opportunities. Kayakers come from all over the country to paddle in the surrounding area. Plenty of rainfall and dam releases allow for year round paddling. Learning to kayak is a serious undertaking and is very rewarding. Professional instruction should be obtained before venturing out on the open water for the first time. Below is a list of kayaking schools in the area.

Adventour- 1-888-574-TOUR.
North American River Runners- 1-800-950-2585.
Wildwater Expeditions Unlimited- 1-800-WVA RAFT.

Rock Climbing- The New River Gorge has some of the best rock climbing in the country. Miles of sandstone cliff high above the river provide thousands of challenging rock climbs. Climbers from all over the country travel to the New to experience the diversity of rock climbs. Rock climbing and rappelling are dangerous activities and novices should seek professional instruction. Below is a listing of the two guide services in the area that specialize in rock climbing instruction.

Hard Rock- (304) 574-0735. Fayetteville, WV.
New River Mountain Guides- Accredited by the American Mountain Guides Association. 1-800-73-CLIMB or (304) 574-3872. Fayetteville, WV.

Mountain Biking- Many of the trails in this book are ideal for mountain biking. These trails offer a wide variety of riding conditions ranging from railroad grades to rugged single track. Clean drinking water is nonexistent on trails so always bring water. Some trails are closed to bikes so please obey restrictions to avoid conflicts with the park system. There are several local retail bike shops in the area that offer rentals, shuttles and guided bike trips.

Appalachian Sport- Marlington, WV. (304) 799-4050.
Elk River Touring Center- Slatyfork, WV. (304) 572-3771.
Greenbrier Mountain Biking Center- Caldwell, WV. 1-800-571-7102.
Greenbrier River Company- Near Alderson, WV. 1-800-775-2203.
Pedals and Spokes- Beckley, WV. (304) 255-6005.
Ridge Rider- Fayetteville, WV. 1-800-890-2453 or (304) 574-2453.
Woods, Water and Wheels- Lewisburg, WV. (304) 645-5200.

Cross Country Skiing- The higher elevation of the Cranberry Area makes it an excellent choice for winter cross-country skiing. Trips ranging from one day to multi-day excursions are possible. Trails at the New River Gorge and Greenbrier Trail are skiable but only during periods of very heavy snowfall. The lower elevations of the New receive more rain and higher temperatures during the winter. Winter camping is serious and one should be prepared for extreme conditions. Temperatures may drop to -25 F in the Cranberry Area.

This chart shows the optimum conditions for rafting, mountain biking, hiking, climbing and cross-country skiing throughout the year.

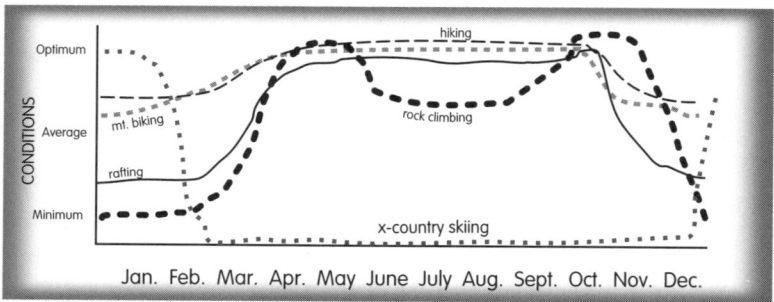

Other Areas

Adjacent to the New River Gorge is the Gauley River National Recreation Area. This is a beautiful and undeveloped area that currently has no developed trail system. The easiest way to access the area is a river trip. Contact one of the local rafting outfitters to arrange a trip. It is also possible to access a small section of the Gauley from the Carnifex Ferry Battlefield State Park. South of Hinton is the Bluestone National Scenic River and north of the New River Gorge is Summersville Lake. Closer to the Cranberry Area is Watoga State Park, Greenbrier State Forest, Calvin Price State Forest and a large section of the Monongahela National Forest. All of these areas contain excellent trails and camping facilities.

Camping and Accommodations

Below is a list of campgrounds and other accommodations in the area . In the New River Gorge, camping is permitted on Park Service land but you must be at least 100 feet from the edge of the cliff, roads and streams. Keep in mind that not all land in the New River Gorge is owned by the Park Service. Much of the land is private property. The majority of camping areas are open on a seasonal basis (usually April-October). It is recommended that you call in advance for commercial campgrounds. Park Service campgrounds are free.

New River Gorge National Park Service Campgrounds

These are primitive campgrounds (no fee) with limited facilities open year round on a first-come, first-served basis. Camping is permitted on Park Service land but you must be at least 100 feet away from the cliff top, streams, roads, trails, parking areas, historical ruins, etc.

Stone Cliff- Located one mile upstream of Dunglen Day Use Area near Thurmond.

Glade Creek- Located near the trailhead of the Glade Creek Trail.

Army Camp and Grandview Sandbar- Located near Grandview.

State Park and State Forest Campgrounds

Babcock State Park- Fee campground with tent or trailer sites and full facilities located off WV 41, near the town of Clifftop. Cabin rentals are also available. Phone (304) 438-3003.

Greenbrier State Forest- Near Lewisburg. (304) 536-1944.

Seneca State Forest- Located south of Cass near the Greenbrier Trail.

Watoga State Park- Located on the Greenbrier Trail south of Marlington.

Cranberry Wilderness Camping Areas

All campgrounds are provided with toilet facilities and hand pumps for water. Each site has a picnic table, fireplace and parking area. Electricity, firewood and trailer hookups are not provided.

Summit Lake- 10 miles east of Richwood on Rt. 39/55. Open March 15-Dec. 1. Daily fee is $5.

Big Rock- 6 miles north on Forest Road 76 north of Rt. 39/55. March 15-Dec.1. Daily fee $5 to $8.

Cranberry Campground- Located on Forest Road 76 about 7 miles north east of Big Rock Campground. Sites range from $5 to $8 a day.

Bishop Knob- Located on Forest Road 101. Access from Big Rock Campground or from Rt. 46. Open April 1 to Dec.1. Daily fee $2.

Tea Creek Campground- Located on Forest Road 86 about one mile north of Highland Scenic Highway. Open all year. Very nice camping area.

Commercial Campgrounds

Chestnut Creek Campground-
Near Fayetteville. (304) 574-3136.
Greenbrier River Campground-
Near Alderson. 1-800-775-2203.
Mountain River Campground-
Near Fayetteville. (304) 658-5266.
Mountain State Outdoor Campground-
Near Fayetteville. (304) 574-0947.
New River Gorge Campground-
Near Fayetteville. (304) 658-9926.
North American River Runners Campground- Near Fayetteville. 1-800-950-2585.
Riftrafters- Near Fayetteville. (304) 574-0413.
The River Retreat Campground-
Near Fayetteville. (304) 658-4530.

Bed and Breakfast Inns

Dogwood Ridge Farms- Hico, WV.
(304) 658-4396.
Edelweiss Inn- Beaver, WV. (304) 763-3391.
Foxwood Bed and Breakfast-
(304) 466-5514.
Garvey House- Winona, WV. (304) 574-3235.
Grandview Bed and Breakfast- Beaver, WV.
(304) 763-4381.
Heritage House- Hinton, WV.
(304) 466-6070.
Historic Brock House- Summersville, WV.
(304) 872-4887.
Jerico Bed and Breakfast- Marlington, WV.
(304) 799-6241.
Jones House Bed and Breakfast- Hinton, WV.
(304) 466-2108.
Morris Harvey House- Fayetteville, WV.
(304) 574-1179.
Old Clark Inn- Marlington, WV.
1-800-849-4184.
Rocky Gap Bed and Breakfast- White Sulphur Springs, WV. (304) 536-1874.
Sunset- Hinton, WV. (304) 466-3740.
White Horse Bed and Breakfast-
Fayetteville, WV. (304) 574-1400.
Woodcrest Bed and Breakfast-
Beckwith, WV. (304) 574-3870.

Cabin Rentals

Driftwood Lodge- Mt. Nebo, WV.
(304) 872-4442.
Eagle Rock- Hinton, WV. (304) 466-0736.
Farmhouse in Green Pastures- Ghent, WV.
(304) 787-3009.
High Meadow Farm Lodge- Wolf Creek, WV.
(304) 445-7684.
Jenny's Cottage- Nimitz, WV.
(304) 466-0548.
Lick Creek Valley Farm- Green Sulphur Springs, WV. (304) 466-3844.
Mill Creek Cabins- Lansing, WV.
(304) 658-5005.
Mountain Chalets- Fayetteville, WV.
(304) 465-3622.
O'possum Creek Retreat- Lansing, WV.
(304) 574-4836.
Vanishing Creek Cabins- Lansing, WV.
(304) 465-8882.

Motels, Resorts and Lodges

Beckley Hotel- Beckley, WV. (304) 252-8661.
Best Western Four Seasons- Beckley, WV.
(304) 252-0671.
Budget Inn- White Sulphur Springs, WV.
(304) 536-2121.
Comfort Inn- Fayetteville, WV.
(304) 574-3443.
Days Inn- Beckley, WV. (304) 255-5291.
Glade Springs Resort- Daniels, WV.
(304) 763-2000.
The Greenbrier Resort- White Sulphur Springs, WV. (304) 536-1110.
Hawk's Nest- Ansted, WV (304) 658-5196.
Holiday Inn- Oak Hill, WV. (304) 465-0571.
Pipestem Resort State Park- (304) 466-1800.

Restaurants

Bazils- Fayetteville, (304) 574-2777
Breeze Hill- Fayetteville, (304) 574-0436
Cathedral Cafe- Fayetteville, (304) 574-0202
Chef Dan's- Hico, (304) 658-5276.
Fat Tire Deli- Fayetteville, (304) 574-0599.
Food & Friends- Lewisburg, (304) 645-4548.
Hawk's Nest- Ansted, (304) 658-5212.
PacosTacos-Take-out , Fayetteville.
Sedona Grill- Fayetteville, (304) 574-3411.
Smokey's Grill- Fayetteville, (304) 574- 4905.

Outdoor Equipment Stores

Backcountry- Main street, Fayetteville, WV. 1-877-226-8754.
Blue Ridge Outdoors- Hiking, camping, climbing, outdoor clothing and equipment. Fayetteville, WV. (304) 574-2425.
Elk River Touring Center- Slatyfork, WV. (304) 572-3771.
Four Seasons- Richwood, WV. (304) 846-2862.
Woods, Water and Wheels- Mountain Bikes, bike equipment and services. Lewisburg, WV. (304) 645-5200.
Pedals and Spokes- Beckley, WV. 1-888-548-6005
Ridge Rider Mountain Bikes- Mountain bikes, bike equipment and services. Fayetteville, WV. (304) 574-BIKE.
Starkk Moon Kayaks- Fayetteville, WV. (304) 574-2550

Emergency Telephone Numbers

Below is a list of hospitals, clinics, ambulance services and law enforcement numbers in the event of an injury or accident.
Ambulance and Fire- Dial 911.
State Police in West Virginia- 1-800-WVA-WVSP or 911.
New River Gorge National River- 911
Gauley River Ranger Station- Richwood, WV. (304) 846-2695.
Plateau Medical Center- Oak Hill, WV. (304) 469-8600.
Raleigh General Hospital- Beckley, WV. Emergency Room-(304) 256-4180.
Columbia Greenbrier Valley Medical Center- Lewisburg, WV. (304) 647-6080.
Pocahontas Memorial Hospital, Marlington- (304) 799-7400.

Safety Tips
• Never leave valuables in your car. Take them with you or lock valuables in the trunk of your car while hiking. Never leave valuables in a car parked overnight.
• Be aware of poison ivy. This vine is common in the forests of West Virginia.
• The only poisonous animals in the area are rattlesnakes and copperheads. Always watch where you walk and place your hands.
• Mountain bikers should ride on open trails only and should yield trail to hikers and animals.

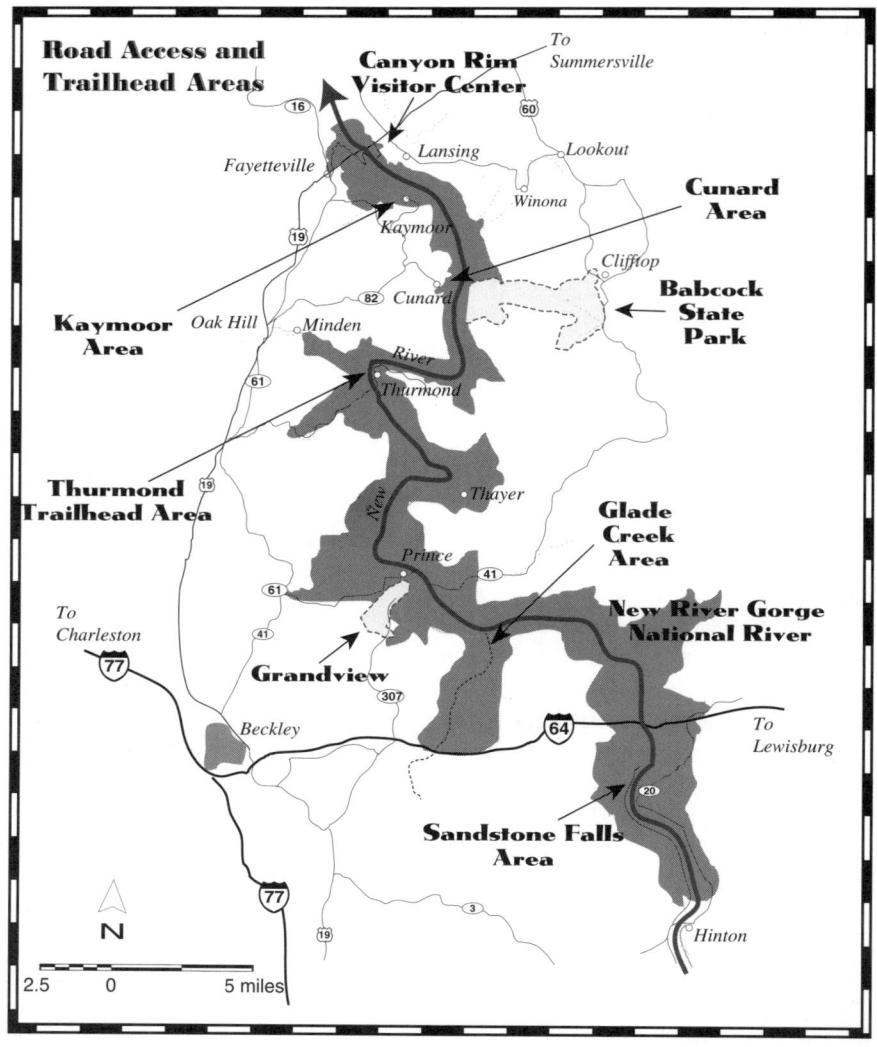

The map above shows the area covered in Chapter One. Main trailhead area locations and road access are shown. Trails are listed from the top of the page starting at the Canyon Rim Visitor Center and described as one would travel upstream or south.

Chapter 1

· New River Gorge ·

It is on this stretch of river that the New unleashes its fury in a long and sustained series of rapids. It is also along this section of river that the sandstone cliffs one thousand feet above the river have formed miles of unbroken cliffline up to one hundred fifty feet high. These cliffs are known throughout the country and the world for their excellent rock climbing. The country roads, old logging roads, and trails weaving in and out of the Gorge provide mountain bikers with a range of possibilities. Many of the trails in this section are accessed from the Fayetteville area or near Cunard and Thurmond. Babcock State Park (Chapter 2) is located across the river from Cunard Station but the main access is from Route 60 on the northern rim of the Gorge.

The areas most noteworthy man-made landmark is the massive bridge that crosses the New River near Fayetteville. There are several overlooks and trails that allow close-up views of this massive structure. An interesting and informative history is displayed in the Canyon Rim Visitor Center adjacent to the bridge on the north side of the rim.

The upper section (Hinton to Cunard) of the river is not as wild as the lower section and contains idyllic stretches of calm water interspersed with several rapids. Cunard Station is the main put-in for rafters and boaters running the Lower New River and Cunard is also the trailhead for several popular hiking and biking trails. Upstream (south) of Cunard is the old town of Thurmond. The Park Service is currently in the process of restoring parts of this town. The Dunglen Day Use area is located across the river from Thurmond and provides picnic facilities and a boat launch for the public. Several miles upstream of Thurmond is the canyon rim Grandview Park. This park has a selection of short trails that offer excellent views of the Gorge plus picnic facilities for the days outing. Continuing upstream is the Glade Creek Trail Area. This is one of the more remote and scenic areas in the Gorge. Further upstream, several miles north of Hinton, is Sandstone Falls and Brooks Falls. This is the southern most extent of the New River Gorge National Scenic River.

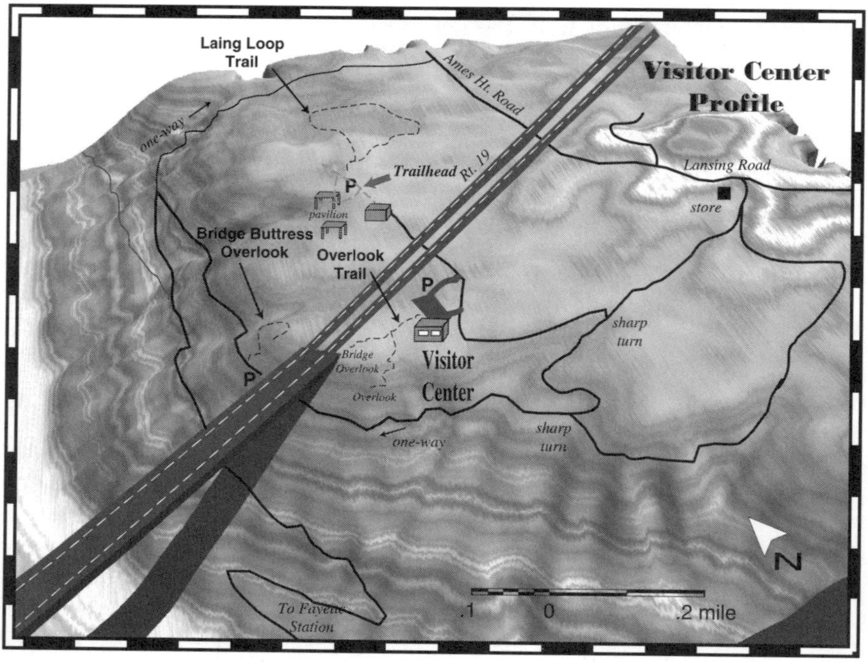

Laing Loop

Length- 1.1 miles RT.
Difficulty- Easy.
Elev. Change- 50 ft.
Points of Interest- Casual walk through nice forest.
Condition- Maintained. *Map* (p. 18)

Laing Loop Trail Description - From the gravel parking area, 75 yards beyond the building, enter the forest at the Laing Loop Trailhead sign. The trail goes through forests, open fields and rhododendron thickets. Very easy hiking on flat terrain.

> **Note:**
> Fayette Station Road is one-way from the north (Visitor Center) to south (Fayetteville).

Canyon Rim Overlook Boardwalk

Length- 0.1 mile OW.
Difficulty- Easy.
Elev. Change- 150 ft.
Points of Interest- Interesting close-up view of the Bridge and Gorge. Canyon Rim Visitor Center.
Condition- Maintained. *Map* (p. 18)

How To Get There- The trailhead for the boardwalk is located at the Visitors Center off Rt. 19 on the north side of the bridge. The Laing Loop Trailhead is also located on the north side of the bridge in the Burnwood Day Use Area directly across Rt. 19 from the visitor center.

Boardwalk Trail Description - For the Boardwalk Trail, park in the visitor center parking area and follow the paved sidewalk that leads west, (away from the Visitor Center). Drop down a long flight of wooden stairs to a dramatic overlook of the Gorge and the Bridge. There is also a nice view of the Bridge from another small overlook located above Rt. 19 approximately 75 yards beyond the first flight of stairs leading down to the overlook. It is also a good idea to visit the Visitor Center. There are informative displays describing the history, natural geology and animal life in the area. The National Park Service often presents slide shows and films throughout the summer and sponsors informative hikes and presentations.

Bridge Buttress Overlook

Length- 0.1 mile RT.
Difficulty- Moderate. Requires some scrambling.
Elev. Change- 150 ft.
Points of Interest- Interesting close-up view of the Bridge and Gorge. Very nice scenic overlook. Rock climbers and rappellers.
Condition- Maintained. *Map* (p. 18)

How To Get There- From the Visitor Center continue down Fayette Station Road (Rt. 16). There are two hairpin turns so if you are driving a van or camper it is best to take the longer route via Lansing Road. Park at the parking area under the bridge .

Trail Description - This is a short hike up to the top of the Bridge Buttress climbing area. From the parking area, walk down the road to the wood steps. The stairs lead from the road up to the base of the cliff. Follow the trail to the left staying at the base of the cliff until you reach a small gully. Scramble up the gully then turn right and follow the trail out to the overlook. *Use caution!*

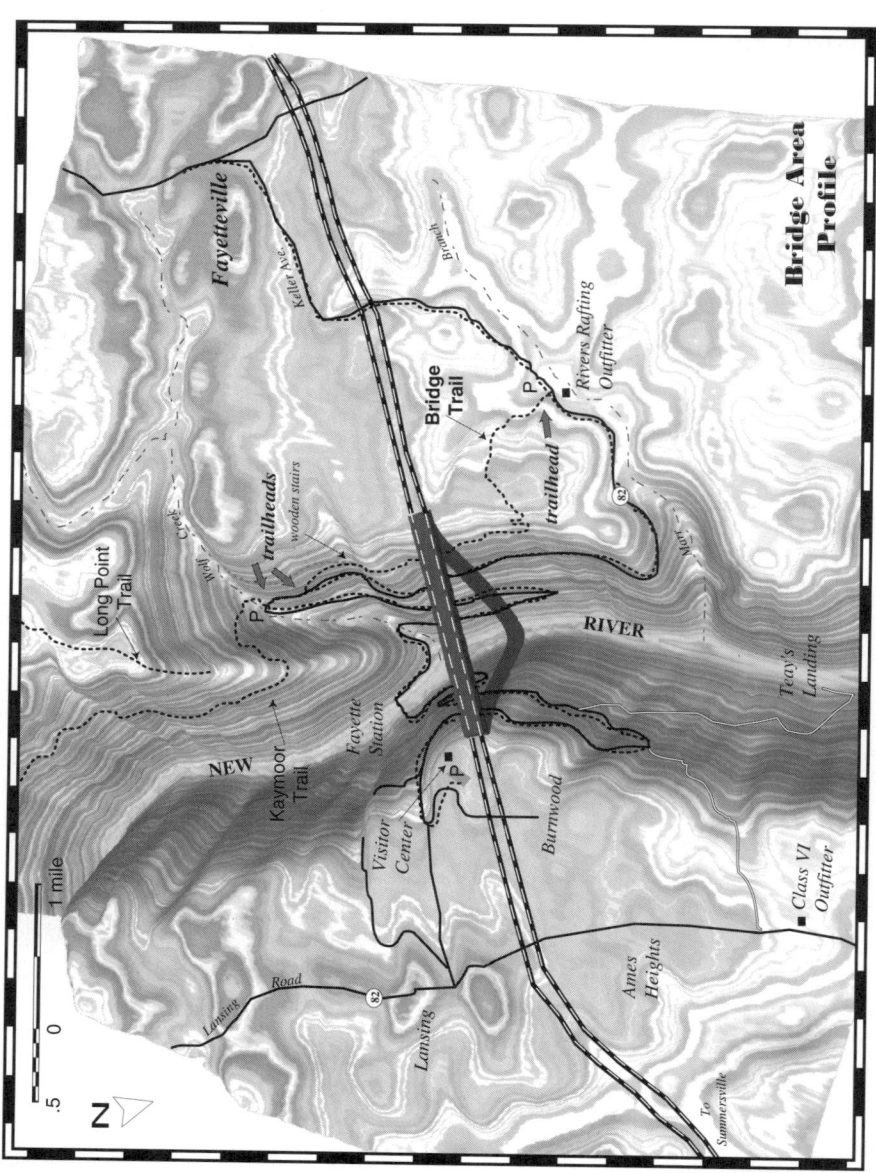

Bridge Area Profile

Long Point Trail

Fayetteville

Keller Ave.

Wolf Creek

Branch

trailheads

wooden stairs

Bridge Trail

Rivers Rafting Outfitter

P

P

trailhead

82

Kaymoor Trail

NEW

Fayette Station

RIVER

Marr

Teay's Landing

Visitor Center

P

Burnwood

Lansing Road

Lansing

82

Ames Heights

Class VI Outfitter

To Summersville

N

1 mile

.5   0

Gorge Ride

Length- 7 miles OW.
Difficulty- Strenuous.
Elev. Change- 900 ft.
Points of Interest- Bridge, Fayette Station.
Condition- Paved road. *Map-* (p. 20)

How To Get There- The most convenient starting points is the Canyon Rim Visitor Center.

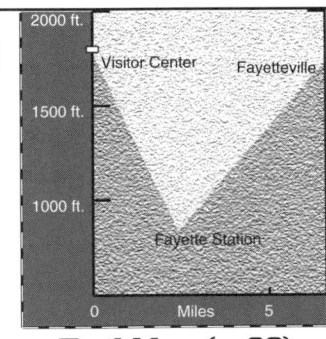

Trail Map- (p. 20)

Description - Enjoy the long downhill ride from the Visitor Center to Fayette Station. The road is one-way from the Visitor Center. Cross the newly reconstructed bridge then begin the long strenuous ascent up the other side of the Gorge. The bridge at the bottom is a replica of the old bridge that was demolished in 1998. Fayette Station is a great place to watch kayakers and rafters run the last big rapid on the river. It's also a nice place for a swim on hot days.

New River Bridge Trail

Length- 1.5 miles OW.
Difficulty- Moderate.
Elev. Change- 350 ft.
Points of Interest- Interesting view of the Bridge.
Condition- Maintained. *Map* (p. 20)
Connections- Connect with Fayetteville Trail.

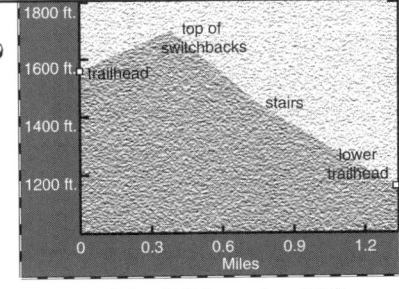

Trail Map- (p. 20)

How To Get There- There are two trailheads for this trail. The first is located approximately 0.8 miles down the Fayette Station Road across from Rivers Rafting Company. The second is located 30 yards up the road from the Kaymoor Trail parking area.

Trail Description- Most people prefer to start at the upper trailhead across from Rivers. This makes the trail a downhill hike. From the upper parking area trailhead, follow the trail across the field and uphill. The trail enters the forest and begins to descend a series of steep switchbacks. Continue, passing directly underneath the Bridge. At the intersection and stairs, take the left fork down to the parking area. It is also possible to take the right fork and continue out to Long Point (Fayetteville trail)

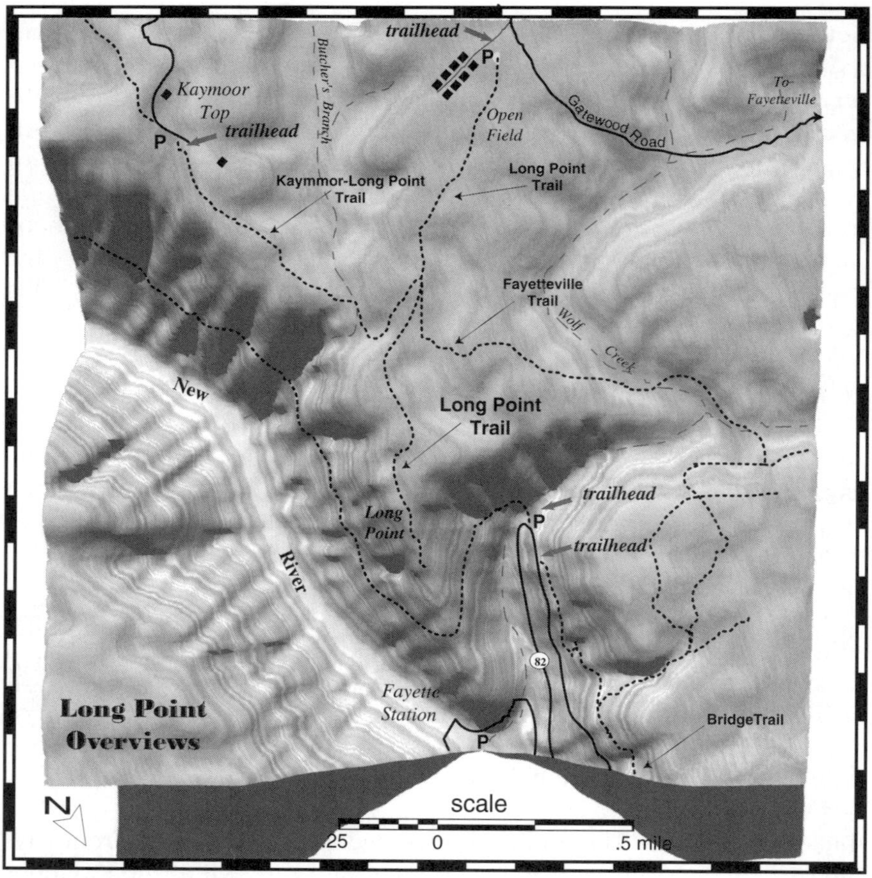

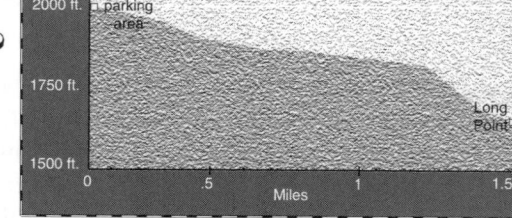

The map shows the Long Point Overviews area with the following labels:

- trailhead
- Kaymoor Top trailhead / P
- Butcher's Branch
- Open Field
- Gatewood Road
- To Fayetteville
- Kaymmor-Long Point Trail
- Long Point Trail
- Fayetteville Trail / Wolf Creek
- Long Point Trail
- Long Point
- trailhead / P
- trailhead
- New River
- 82
- Fayette Station / P
- Bridge Trail
- Long Point Overviews
- N
- scale .25 0 .5 mile

Long Point Trail

Length- 3 miles RT.
Difficulty- Easy.
Elev. Change- 300 ft.
Points Of Interest- Unique panoramic view of the New River Gorge and Bridge from trails end.
Condition- Maintained.
Connections- Connection with the Fayetteville Trail.

Elevation profile: 2000 ft. parking area — 1750 ft. — 1500 ft.; Miles 0 to 1.5; Long Point

Trail Map- (p. 22)

How To Get There- To reach the trailhead, turn left onto Gatewood Road after driving southwest through Fayetteville on Rt. 16. Follow Gatewood for 1.8 miles and turn left at an old school bus shed onto a dead end paved road. If you drive past the Kaymoor No. 1 sign, you've gone too far. Trailhead parking is on the left.

Trail Description- The Long Point Trail is an easy hike out to a spectacular view of the New River Gorge and bridge. The trail follows an old road bed for most of the hike with the last several hundred yards becoming a very narrow path. From the parking area, follow the trail across the old baseball diamond. After several hundred yards the trail enters the forest. Enter the forest and continue following the main trail. At one point an intersection is reached where it is possible to linkup with the Fayetteville Trail. If you follow the right branch, the trail will take you to the Kaymoor Parking Area. Turning left here will take you to the New River Bridge Trail. Stay on the main trail. The total time for this hike at a leisurely pace is about 1 1/2 hours.

Kaymoor-Long Point Trail

Length- 1.5 miles OW.
Difficulty- Easy.
Elev. Change- 250 ft.
Points of Interest- Kaymoor site, panoramic views from Long Point of the New River and Bridge
Condition- Maintained. *Map-* (p. 22)
Connections- Connect with Fayetteville Trail and Long Point Trail.

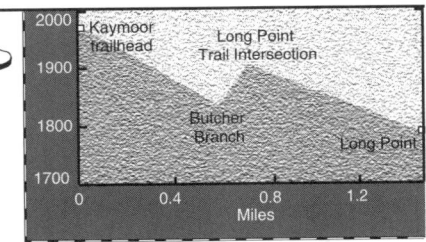

Trail Map- (p. 22)

How To Get There- The trailhead is located at Kaymoor Top. From Fayetteville, follow Gatewood Road 1.9 miles and turn left at the Kaymoor No. 1 Sign. Follow this road one mile and park at the established parking area.

Trail Description- From the parking area, continue walking down the road 25 yards and turn right onto the trail. Follow the trail through an over grown field then down a steep embankment to a hemlock forest. The trail forks here in the hemlock forest. Take the left fork, cross over a small stream and then turn right. Continue following this trail up a gradual incline to its intersection with the Long Point Trail. Turn right at this intersection to reach Long Point. Long Point is another 20-30 minute walk.

Bridge Trail-Long Point Trail (Fayetteville Trail)

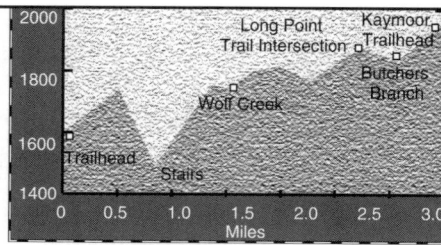

Length- 3 miles OW.
Difficulty- Moderate.
Elev. Change- 400 ft.
Points of Interest- Interesting view of the Bridge.
Condition- Partially maintained.
Connections- Connect with Long Point-Kaymoor Top Trail.

Trail Map- (p. 22, 24)

How To Get There- This trail is actually two trails combined. The trailhead is located on the right 0.8 miles off Rt. 19 on the old Fayette Station Road directly across from Rivers Rafting Company. Alternate starts are Kaymoor Top or the hairpin turn parking area for the Kaymoor Trail.

Trail Description- From the parking area, follow the trail uphill. The trail soon begins a steep descent down several switchbacks then levels off as it passes under the Bridge. The trail then begins a gradual ascent up a small creek drainage, continue following the trail as it works its way uphill then back down to Wolf Creek. Cross Wolf Creek (no bridge) and continue to the intersection of the Long Point Trail. At the Long Point intersection, turn left and continue out to Long Point or continue to Kaymoor Top from the intersection (profile above). This trail may be difficult to follow in some places.

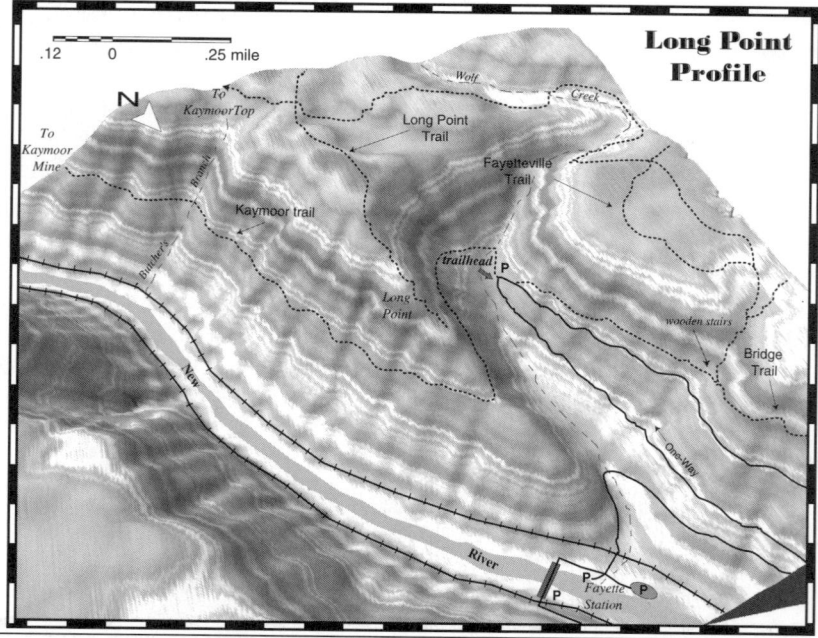

Endless Wall Trail

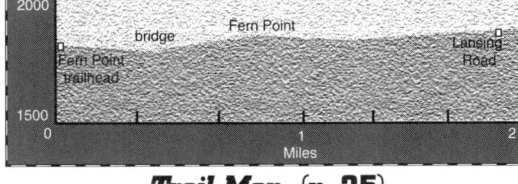

Length- 1.7 miles (OW) from Fern Point parking area to Lansing Road.

Difficulty- Easy.
Elev. Change- 100 ft.

Trail Map- (p. 25)

Points of Interest- Excellent view of the gorge. Rock climbers.
Condition- Maintained. Extension and new parking area planned for 2000.

How To Get There- The trailhead is located at the Fern Point parking area 1.5 miles east of Rt. 19 on Lansing Road.

Trail Description- From the parking area, the trail leads through a beautiful pine forest out to the cliff top passing over a small bridge at Fern Creek. A cliff top trail skirts the entire length of the cliff offering spectacular views of the gorge and river. Several spur trails branch off the main trail and are designated as climber access only. The cliff averages about 100 to 130 feet high so don't get too close to the edge. It is possible to do a loop or just an out and back. The loop puts you on Lansing Road about .5 miles east of the parking area at the top of the hill. This area is heavily used by rock climbers so **do not throw anything off the cliff!** An expansion of this trial will be completed in 2000 making the trail about 2.4 miles long from parking area to parking area.

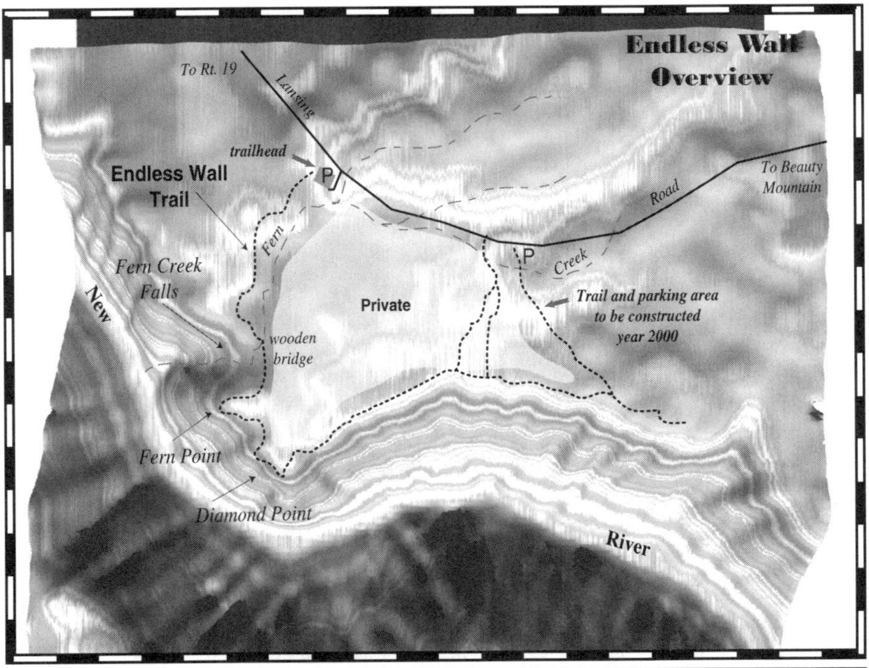

Endless Wall Overview

To Rt. 19

trailhead

Endless Wall Trail

Fern Creek Falls

New

wooden bridge

Private

Fern Point

Diamond Point

Lansing

Creek Road

To Beauty Mountain

Trail and parking area to be constructed year 2000

River

Kaymoor Trail

Length- 4 miles RT.
Difficulty- Easy.
Elev. Change- 420 ft.
Points of Interest- Excellent view of the Gorge. Old Kaymoor mine site.
Condition- Maintained.
Connections- Connect with Kaymoor Miner's Trail or continue to Cunard.

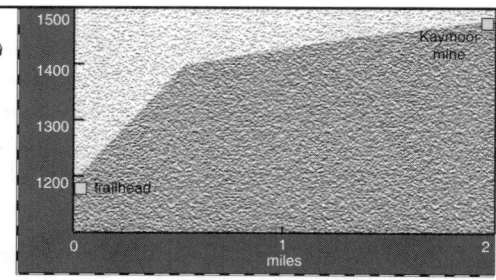

Trail Map- (p. 26, 28)

How To Get There- Starts at the second hairpin turn on the north side of Fayette Station Road.

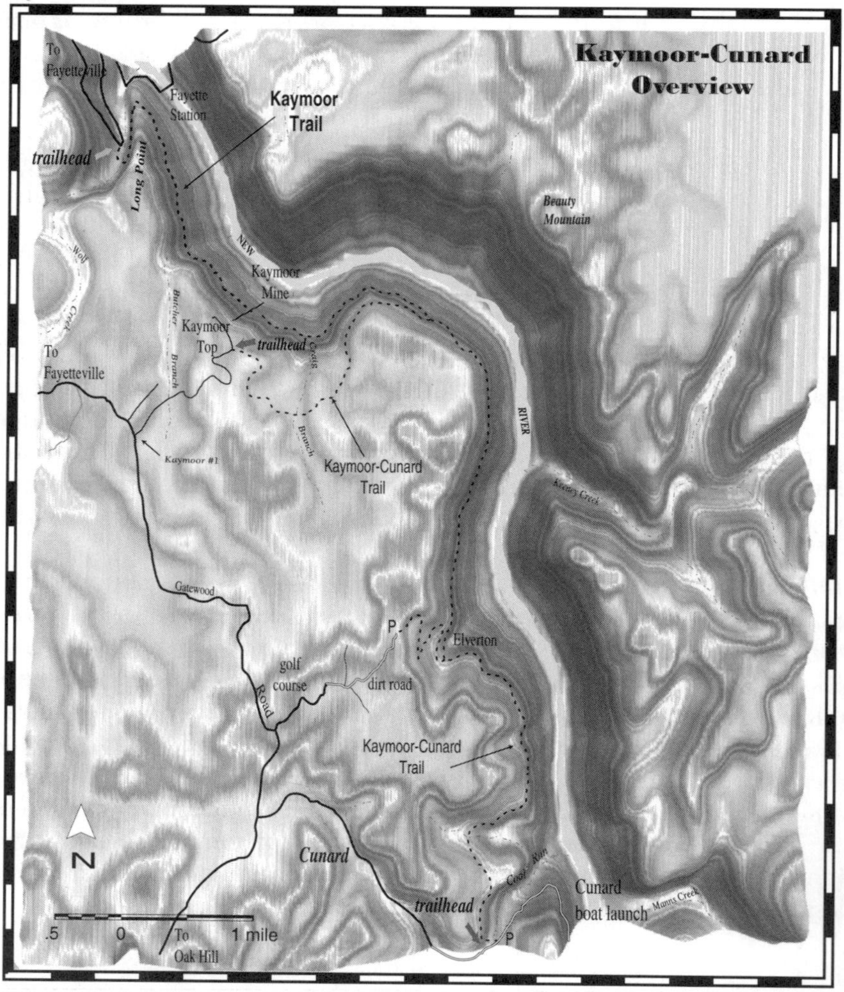

Trail Description- From the parking area walk upstream 50 yards to a small bridge. Cross the bridge and continue up the steep hill and around Long Point. The trail flattens and contours gently to the old mine site. At the mine site it is possible to follow the stairs to the bottom or hike up to Kaymoor Top via the Miner's Trail. It is also possible to continue on to Cunard. Excellent views of the Gorge and easy walking make this a popular trail.

Kaymoor-Cunard Trail

Length- 6.6 miles to Cunard.
3.5 miles to Kaymoor Mine OW.
Difficulty- Moderate.
Elev. Change- 420 ft.
Points of Interest- Excellent view of the Gorge. Old Elverton mine site.
Condition- Maintained.
Connections- Connect with Kaymoor Miner's Trail or Kaymoor Trail.

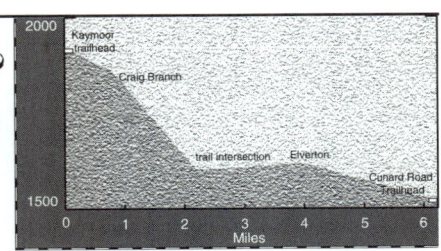

Trail Map- (p. 26, 28)

How To Get There- This trail may be accessed from two separate trailheads. The first trailhead is located at Kaymoor Top. The second is located on the Cunard Road off Salem-Gatewood Road. To reach the Kaymoor trailhead from Fayetteville, take Gatewood road 1.9 miles and turn left at the Kaymoor No. 1 Sign. Follow this road to the National Park Service parking area (approx. one mile). The Cunard trailhead starts from the parking area on the Cunard Access Road. From Fayetteville, take Gatewood Road 4.5 miles and turn left onto the Cunard Road. Drive 2.2 miles following the Cunard Access signs. Soon after crossing a small one-lane bridge the road forks, take a left turn and then another immediate left. This is the Cunard Access Road. The trailhead is on the left approximately one-half mile from the second left turn. The established parking area is on the right.

Trail Description- This trail is very popular with hikers and mountain bikers. From Kaymoor Top, the trail starts at the steel gate. Follow the well maintained road as it eventually drops down through the cliffline and follows the contours of the Gorge while gradually descending. The entire trail is on easy terrain and follows an old road bed offering spectacular views of the Gorge. The trail eventually merges with a second trail. At this intersection, turn left if you are interested in viewing the old Kaymoor Mine (From Kaymoor Top, it is 3.5 miles to the Kaymoor Mine). Hikers may take the Miner's Trail to the top of Kaymoor to complete a loop. Turn right if you want to continue on to Cunard. Continuing to Cunard, you pass the old Elverton Mine and then cross over Coal Run Creek.

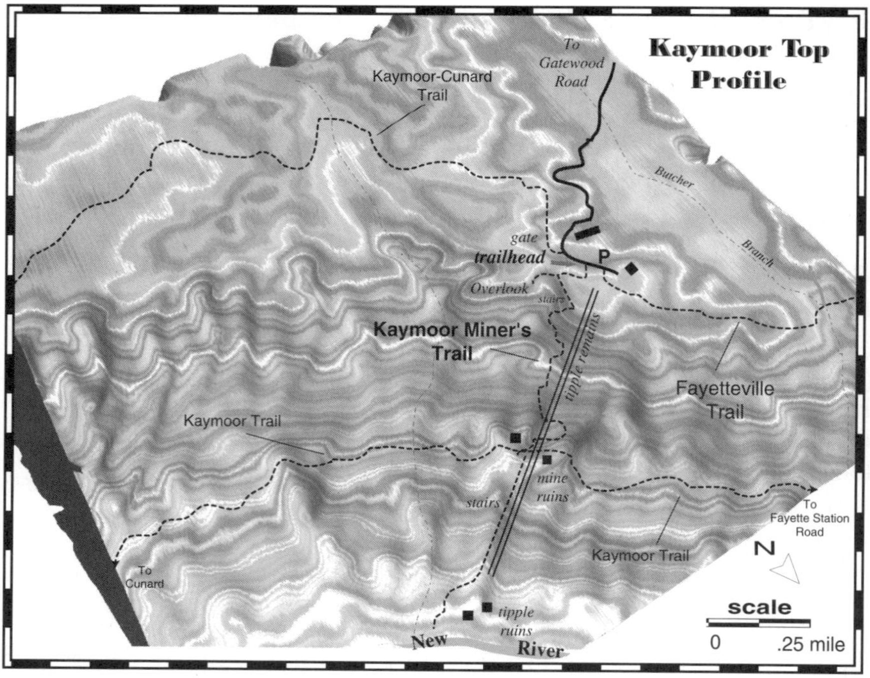

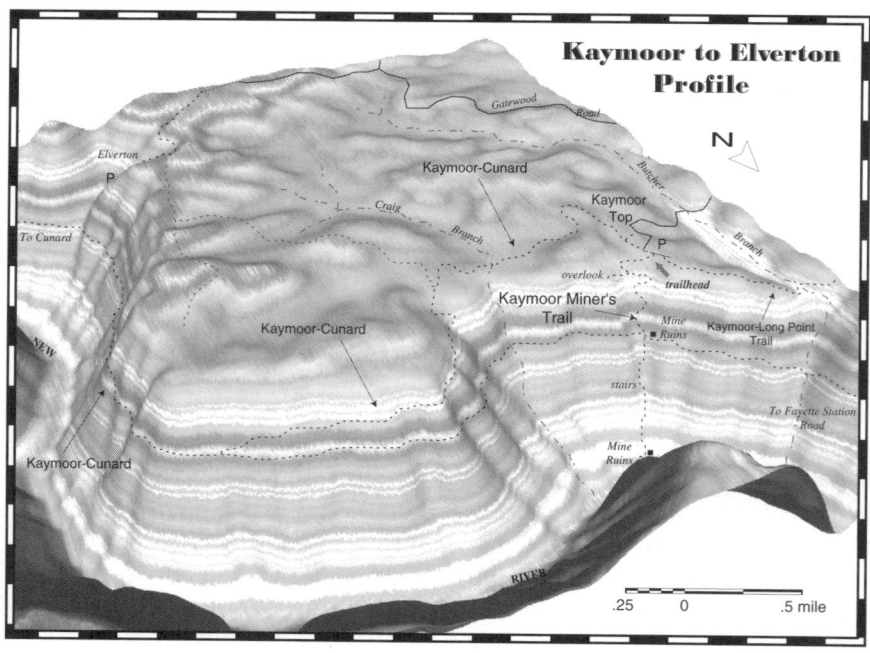

Kaymoor Top Profile

Kaymoor-Cunard Trail

To Gatewood Road

Butcher Branch

gate
trailhead

P

Overlook

stairs

Kaymoor Miner's Trail

tipple remains

Fayetteville Trail

Kaymoor Trail

stairs

mine ruins

Kaymoor Trail

To Fayette Station Road

To Cunard

tipple ruins

New **River**

N

scale

0   .25 mile

Kaymoor to Elverton Profile

N

Gatewood Road

Elverton

P

Butcher Branch

Kaymoor-Cunard

Kaymoor Top

P

To Cunard

Craig Branch

overlook

trailhead

NEW

Kaymoor Miner's Trail

Mine Ruins

Kaymoor-Long Point Trail

Kaymoor-Cunard

stairs

To Fayette Station Road

Kaymoor-Cunard

Mine Ruins

Kaymoor-Cunard

RIVER

.25   0   .5 mile

Kaymoor Miner's Trail

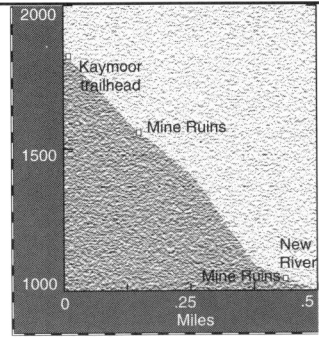

Length- 1 mile RT.
Difficulty- Difficult.
Elev. Change- 400 ft. to midway. 600 ft. to river
Points of Interest- Old Kaymoor Mine ruins and rock climbers.
Condition- Maintained.
Connections- Connect with Kaymoor-Cunard Trail.

Trail Map- (p. 28)

How To Get There- The trailhead is located at Kaymoor Top. From Fayetteville, follow Gatewood Road 1.9 miles and turn left at the Kaymoor No. 1 Sign. Follow this road 1 mile and park at the established parking area.

Trail Description- From the parking area, walk back up the road 40 yards to a small pull-off on the left. The trailhead starts here. (Near the parking area are the remains of the old pulley house that was part of the Kaymoor Mine). Follow the trail as it descends to the cliffline. After the first switchback, there is a spur trail that branches off to the right. A two minute walk will lead you to an excellent overlook of the Gorge and Kaymoor. Continue following the main trail down a short flight of stairs and past a small waterfall. Several steep switchbacks eventually end at an old flight of stairs built for the miners. At this point the Kaymoor Miner's trail intersects the Kaymoor Trail. From this junction, it is possible to return via the Kaymoor-Cunard Trail (turn right) or to hike out to Fayette Station Road via the Kaymoor Trail (left). Continue following the stairs downhill if you wish to see the mine ruins at the bottom of the Gorge. There are about 860 steps to the bottom and just as many on the way up so be prepared!

TARZAN LOOP:
- Start at Kaymoor Top. Run from trailhead down Kaymoor-Cunard Trail to the intersection with the main trail. Turn left and head back to the Kaymoor Mine. Run down the stairs to the river, swim across the river and then back, run back up the stairs all the way to Kaymoor Top. This loop without the swim is called the Jane Loop.

Beauty Mountain Road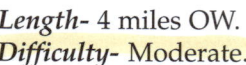

Length- 4 miles OW.
Difficulty- Moderate.
Elev. Change- 100 ft.
Points of Interest- Beauty Mountain Overlook, Visitor Center and country roads.
Condition- Paved with one section of unpaved road. *Map* (p. 30)

How To Get There- Start at the Canyon Rim Visitor Center just off Rt. 19 or the Fern Point parking area on Lansing Road or start at the Overlook.

Trail Description- This ride follows paved road for most of its length. There is one section of unpaved road from the Beauty Mountain Overlook to the intersection with Lansing Road. The paved road is narrow and locals drive fast, be careful. From the Beauty Mountain Overlook it is possible to linkup with the Keeney Creek Trail. To do this continue on the dirt road upstream from the overlook. Stay on the main trail for about one mile as it drops steeply down the Gorge. It comes out on the graveled Keeney Creek Trail.

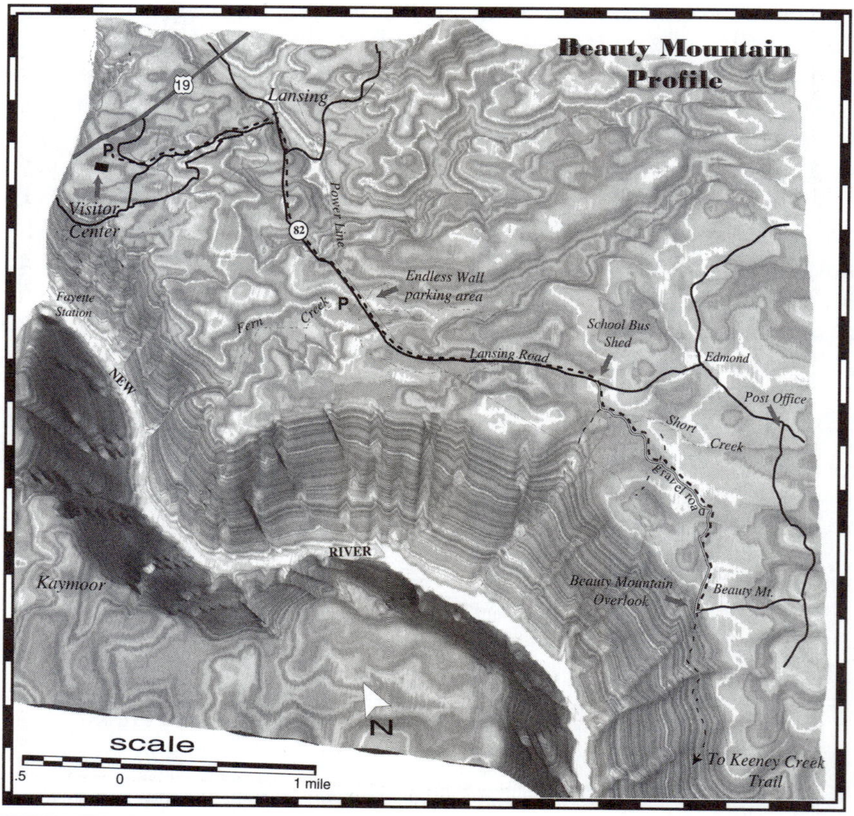

Beauty Mountain Profile

19
Lansing
P.
Visitor Center
82
Power Line
Fayette Station
Fern Creek
Endless Wall parking area
P
Lansing Road
School Bus Shed
Edmond
Post Office
Short Creek
Gravel road
NEW
Kaymoor
RIVER
Beauty Mountain Overlook
Beauty Mt.
N
scale
.5   0   1 mile
To Keeney Creek Trail

Sunday Road

Length- 8.5 miles RT.
Difficulty- Moderate.
Elev. Change- 400 ft.
Points of Interest- Scenic countryside.
Condition- Paved Road.

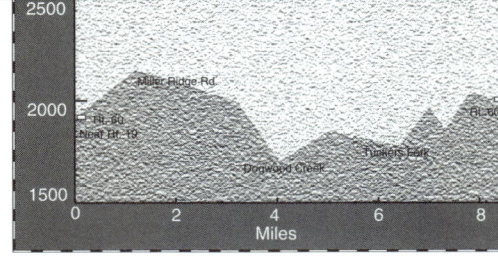

Trail Map- (p. 31)

How To Get There- Start at the pull-off across the abandoned post office in Hico. Nearby is North American River Runners and Mountain River Tours.

Trail Description- This is a paved road loop that passes through some very scenic countryside. The one lane road meanders through farms and open ridges on rolling hills. Rt. 60 is very busy so avoid this section if possible.

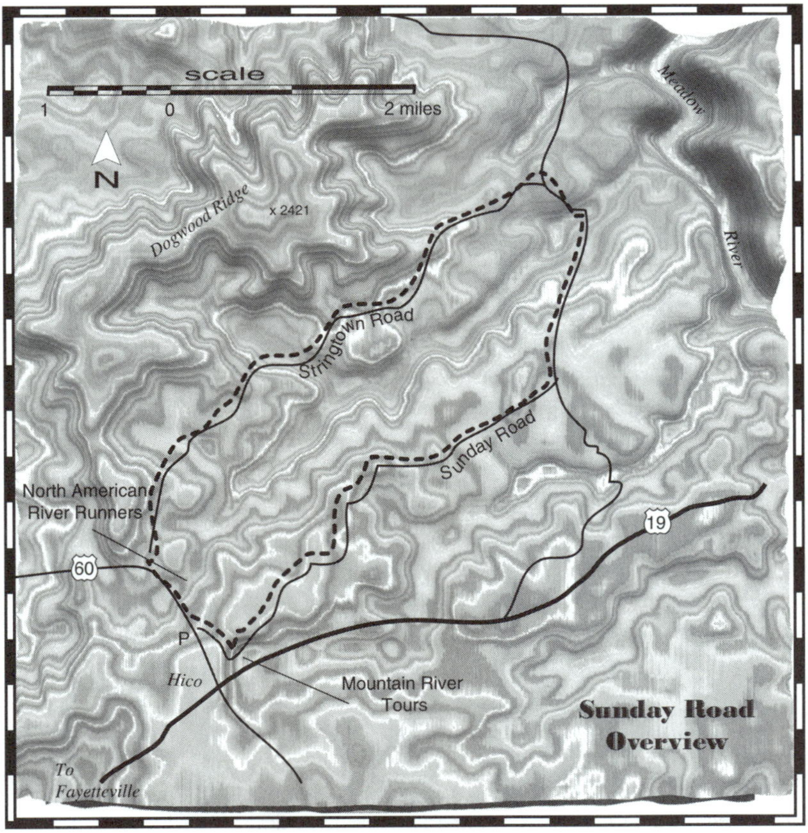

Sunday Road Overview

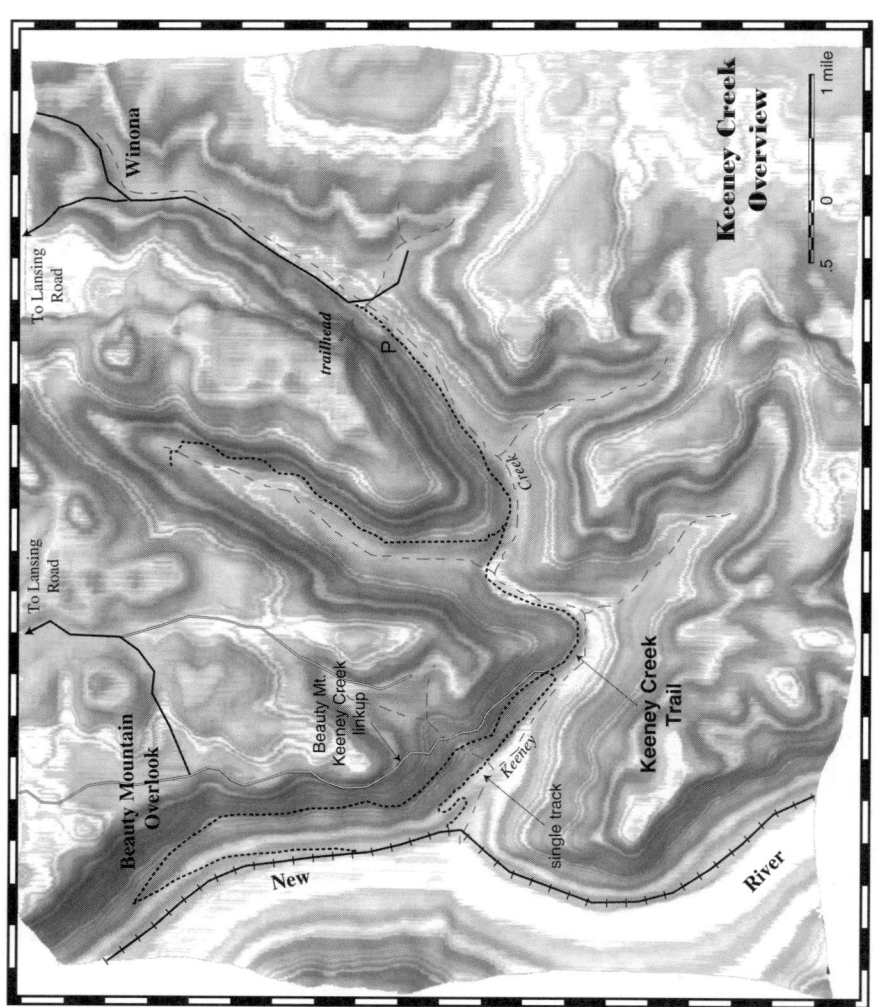

Keeney Creek
Overview

Winona

To Lansing Road

To Lansing Road

trailhead

P

Creek
Creek

Beauty Mt.
Keeney Creek
linkup

**Beauty Mountain
Overlook**

Keeney

single track

**Keeney Creek
Trail**

New

River

.5   0   1 mile

Keeney Creek Trail

Length- 6 miles OW.
Difficulty- Moderate or difficult.
Elev. Change- 900 ft.
Points of Interest- Old access road
to river. Crosses over old railroad
trestles.
Condition- Maintained.
Connections- Possible connection to
Beauty Mountain Overlook.

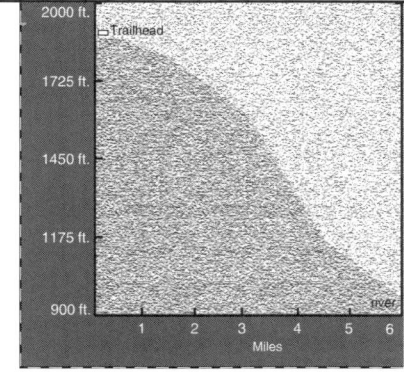

Trail Map- (p. 32, 33)

How To Get There- From Winona continue down the paved road and take a
right onto a gravel road just before reaching a small bridge. Park at the
established parking area (under construction at time of writing).

Trail Description- This trail is very popular with mountain bikers. From
the trailhead it is downhill all the way to the river. Take the former railroad grade all the way down and back up if you want the easier trip. The
cross section map above profiles the railroad grade. Take the direct single
track beside the creek for a more difficult ride to the bottom and then ride
the gradual ascent up the road. The rough single track to the bottom fol-
lowed by graded road to the top is the most popular for bikers. Please
note that the old road on the opposite side of the creek is going to be developed in the near future to allow vehicle access to the bottom.

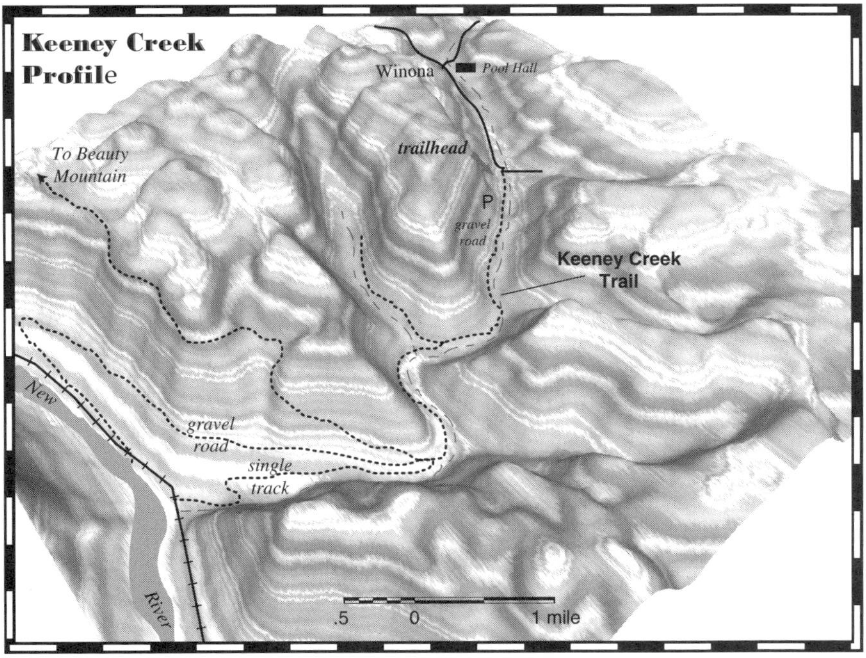

Southside Junction Trail

Length- 6.9 miles OW.
Difficulty- Easy.
Elev. Change- 75 ft.
Points of Interest- Old mining towns, railroad trestles.
Condition- Maintained.
Connections- Thurmond-Minden Trail via Dunloup Creek Trail or Arbuckle Connector.

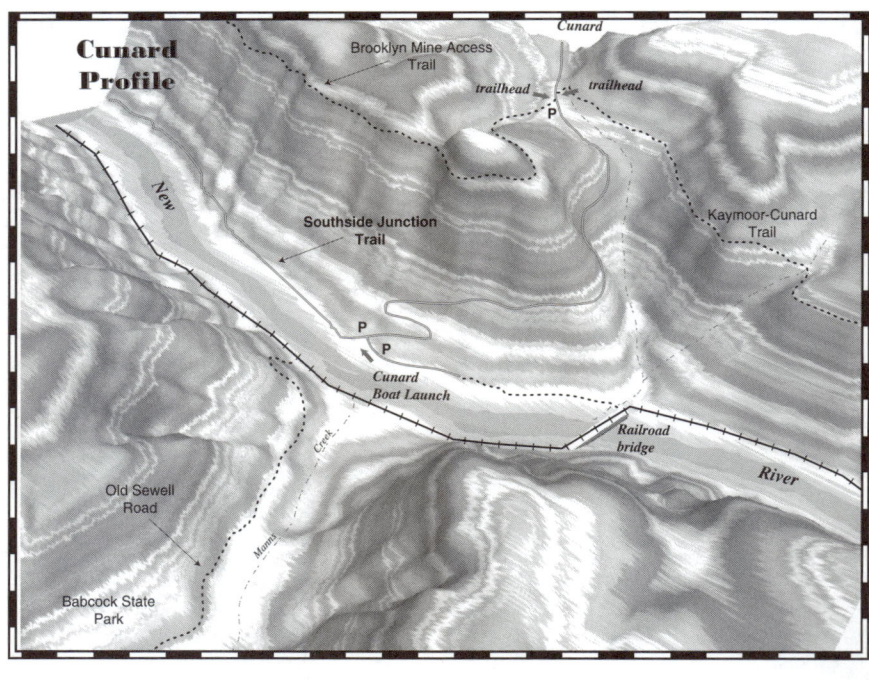

Trail Map- (p. 34, 35)

How To Get There- Trailheads are located at Cunard Road end or across the railroad tracks and parking area at the Dun Glen Day Use Area near Thurmond.

Description - This trail follows an old railroad bed alongside the New River. The hiking is easy and relatively flat. The trail passes through several old mining towns.

Brooklyn Mine Access Trail

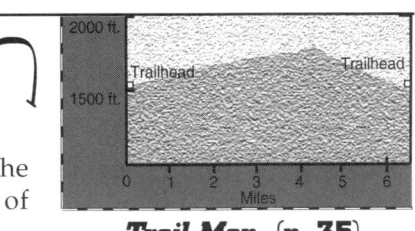

Length- 2 miles OW.
Difficulty- Easy.
Elev. Change- 200 ft.
Points of Interest- Scenic views of the New River Gorge, old mining site of Brooklyn.

Trail Map- (p. 35)

Condition- Maintained. Not recommended for hiking or biking since the trail is used heavily by horses.

How To Get There- The trailhead and parking area is located on the Cunard Access Road about .5 miles after passing through Cunard. The trailhead is on the right side of the road near the parking area.

Description - The Brooklyn Mine Access Trail is one of the few trails designated for equestrian use. The trail follows an old road bed high up the side of the Gorge offering nice views and lush forest. The trail ends at the old Brooklyn Mine site. Double back to return on the same trail. At one time you could drop down the Brooklyn Miner's Trail to the river. This trail is overgrown and difficult to find and not recommended.

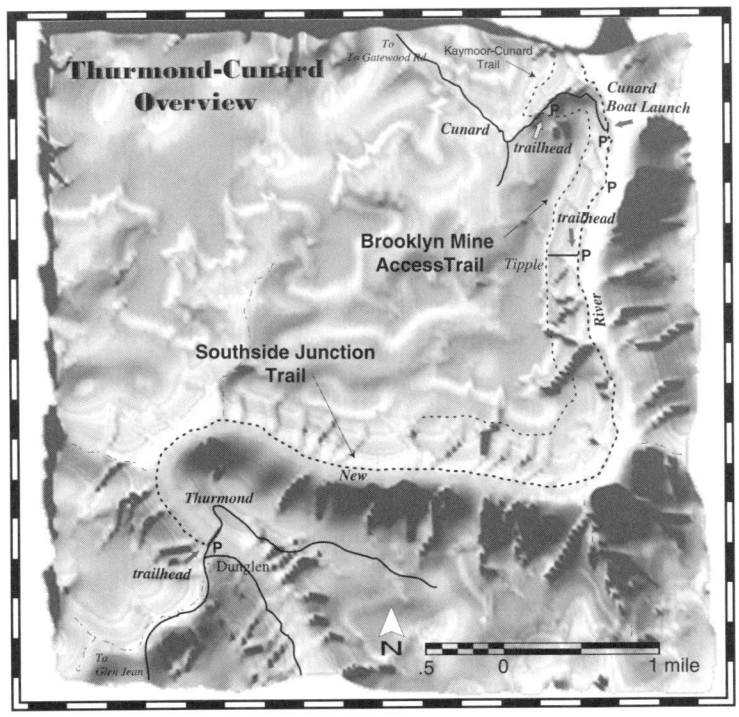

Kaymoor Trail to Thurmond   *Trail Map- (p. 26,35)*

Length- 14 miles OW.
Difficulty- Moderate.
Elev. Change- 600 ft.
Points of Interest- Kaymoor mine site, nice views of Gorge.
Condition- Maintained.
Connections- Connect with Kaymoor-Cunard Trail.

How To Get There- The Kaymoor Trailhead is located on the south side of the gorge at the Kaymoor Trailhead on Fayette Station Road. It is also possible to access the trail from the Kaymoor Miner's Trail or the Kaymoor-Cunard Trail or begin upstream at Thurmond.

Trail Description- This is currently the longest hike in the Gorge and is actually the combination of the Kaymoor Trail to Cunard and then Southside-Junction Trail. The Kaymoor Trail follows an old road bed out to the abandoned Kaymoor Mine Site (see page 27). The first section of the trail is foot traffic only and is known as the Kaymoor Trail. After the Kaymoor mine site, the trail continues upstream connecting with the Kaymoor-Cunard Trail that begins at Kaymoor Top. From this intersection the trail continues on to Cunard where it ends at the Cunard access road. Turn left on the gravel road and drop down to Cunard Station. From Cunard Station take the Southside-Junction Trail to Thurmond. The entire length of trail from the Fayette Station Road to Thurmond has a total length of 14 miles one-way. Mountain bikes are permitted on all sections of the trail except for the section between Kaymoor Mine and Fayette Station Road. To ride the entire trail start or finish at Kaymoor Top. This trail is wide and easy to follow and has excellent views of the New River Gorge. Hikers and bikers can also travel to Thurmond by Amtrack and set out on these trails for a weekend camping trip.

Hiking by the waterfall on the Kaymoor Miner's Trail at Kaymoor.

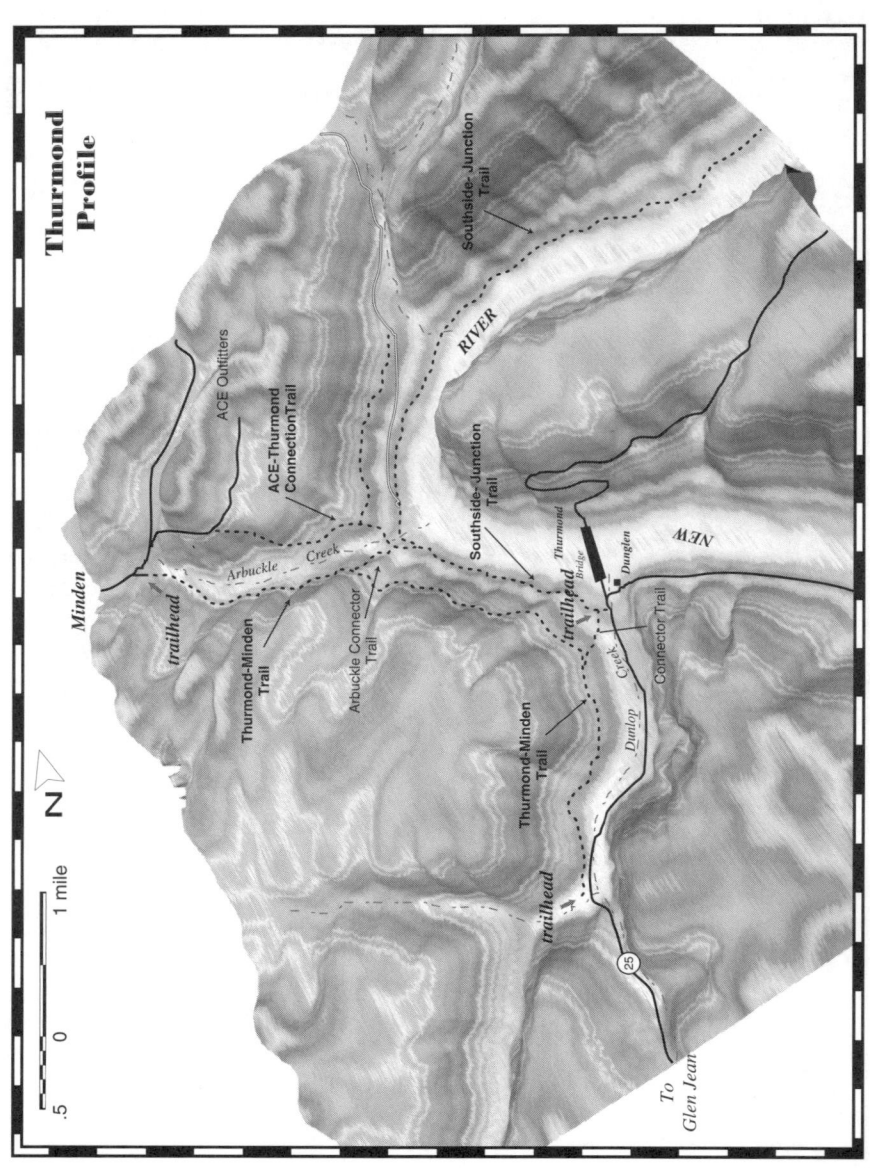

Thurmond Profile

Minden

ACE Outfitters

ACE-Thurmond Connection Trail

Arbuckle Creek

Thurmond-Minden Trail

Arbuckle Connector Trail

trailhead

Southside-Junction Trail

RIVER

Southside-Junction Trail

Thurmond-Minden Trail

trailhead

Thurmond Bridge

Dunlop

Dunglen

NEW

Creek

Connector Trail

trailhead

25

To Glen Jean

N

.5   0   1 mile

Thurmond-Minden Trail

Length- 3.4 miles.
Difficulty- Easy.
Elev. Change- 380 ft.
Points of Interest- Views of Thurmond, railroad trestle bridges.
Condition- Maintained.
Connections- Connect with the Southside-Brooklyn Trail.

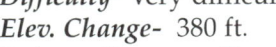

Trail Map- (p. 38)

How To Get There- The most popular starting point is the Thurmond-Minden Trailhead parking area on Rt. 25 near Thurmond. It is also possible to start at the trailhead located in Minden but this is not recommended.

Description - This trail follows an old railroad bed passing several railroad trestle bridges. It follows Dunlop Creek down to Thurmond and then ascends Arbuckle Creek to the town of Minden. There are several excellent overlooks of the old town of Thurmond located on this trail. It is also possible to connect with the South Side Junction to Brooklyn Trail at two points using the Southside Junction to Thurmond-Minden Connector Trail or the Arbuckle Creek To Thurmond-Minden Connector Trail. This is an excellent trail for hiking and biking.

ACE-Thurmond Connection Trail

Length- 3 or 3.5 miles.
Difficulty- Very difficult.
Elev. Change- 380 ft.
Points of Interest- Connector trail.
Condition- Not maintained. Muddy in wet conditions. Not a park trail.
Connections- Connect with the Southside-Brooklyn Trail.

How To Get There- This is a good connection for mountain biking if you ride the Thurmond-Minden trail and want to complete a loop. From the Minden trailhead turn right and then take the second right at the water treatment plant. After about 3/4 miles and just after a sharp left turn look for a logging road on the right that heads downhill. This is the start of the trail. Part of this trail is used for the Captain Thurmond Challenge.

Description - Trail follows the Arbuckle Creek drainage where it eventually forks. Turning right leads to a treacherous downhill where you then wade across a polluted stream to access Arbuckle Connector Trail (Closed to bikes) From here push your bike to Southside-Junction trail. Turning left at the fork continue to a connection with a dirt road that will lead downhill to the Southside-Junction Trail.

Old Town of Thurmond

Thurmond was once the site of a bustling community. Today it sits abandoned on the banks of the New River. It was first settled in the mid 1800's by Captain William Dabney Thurmond. Dabney realized that the New River was a natural corridor linking east to west. Within 50 years his original settlement grew into a hub town for the railroads, mining industry and travelers. By 1873 a railroad line was completed that connected the Ohio River with the James River in Virginia. This artery opened up the vast coal fields of West Virginia. Numerous coal mines sprang up along the New and shipped coal and coke to the industrialized cities of the east. By the late 1800's and early 1900's Thurmond became a bustling depot. Eventually two branch lines were built on Arbuckle Creek and Dunlop Creek (now the Thurmond-Minden Trail). Within years, these two lines would carry over one million tons of coal to Thurmond annually.

By the turn of the century, the town population was about 175. There were three general stores, hotel, several coal mine offices, Western Union Office, drug store, restaurant, one lawyer, and a post office. The town continued to grow and became an important hub for the coal fields, C & O Railway Line and a favorite party town for the miners, train workers and locals. The constant influx of workers and travelers on the railroad line plus the combination of saloons and dance halls earned Thurmond the reputation for a boisterous and rough town. From the early 1900's to the

Looking down Main Street of Thurmond.

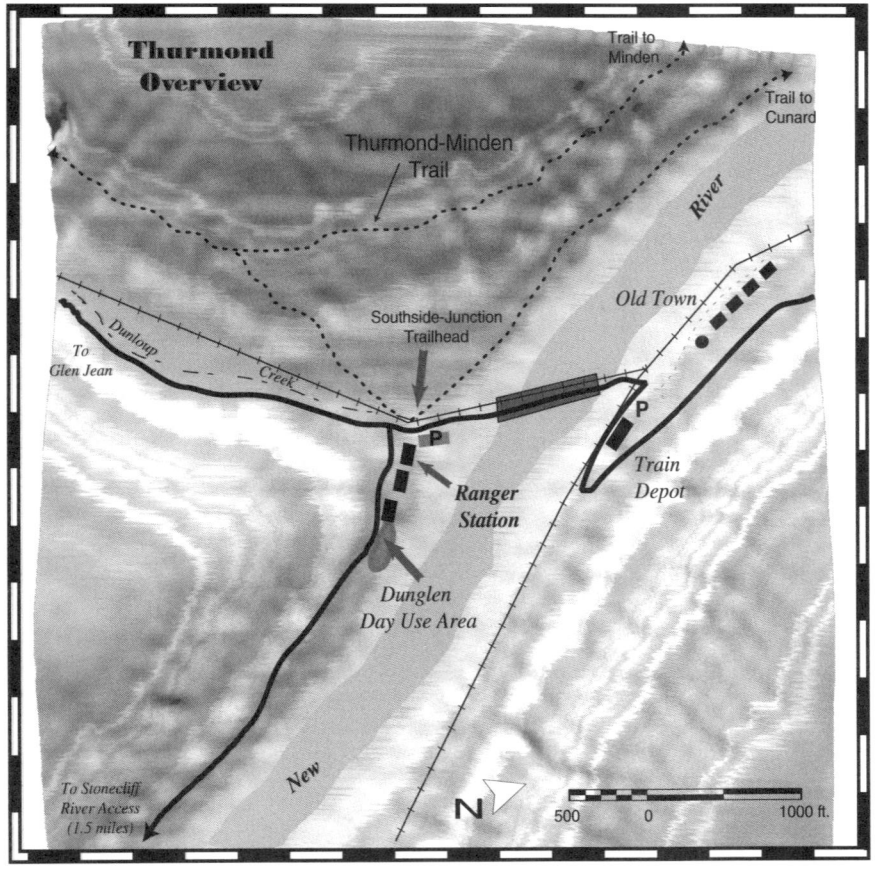

Thurmond Overview

Trail to Minden

Trail to Cunard

Thurmond-Minden Trail

River

Old Town

Southside-Junction Trailhead

Dunloup Creek

To Glen Jean

P

Train Depot

P

Ranger Station

Dunglen Day Use Area

To Stonecliff River Access (1.5 miles)

New

N

500   0   1000 ft.

1930's, the town prospered. By the 1930's the town began a steady decline after a major fire destroyed the impressive Dunglen Hotel, the local bank collapsed and the Armour Meatpacking relocated to Beckley. Since the 1930's the population has dropped from over 400 residents to less than one dozen today. The decrease in dependence on trains and increase in road traffic plus the decline of the mining industry has left Thurmond in the shadow of development.

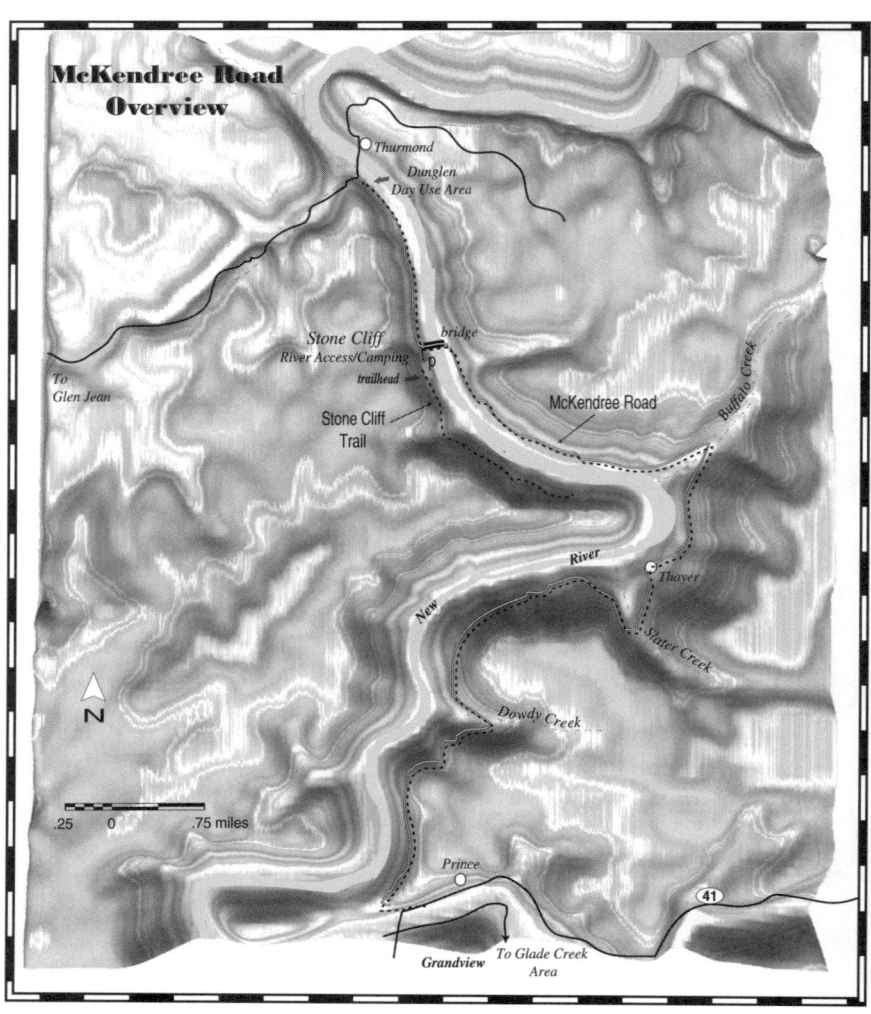

McKendree Road
Overview

Thurmond

Dunglen
Day Use Area

bridge

Stone Cliff
River Access/Camping

trailhead

McKendree Road

Buffalo Creek

To
Glen Jean

Stone Cliff
Trail

River

Thayer

New

Slater Creek

N

Dowdy Creek

.25   0   .75 miles

Prince

41

Grandview   To Glade Creek
Area

McKendree Road

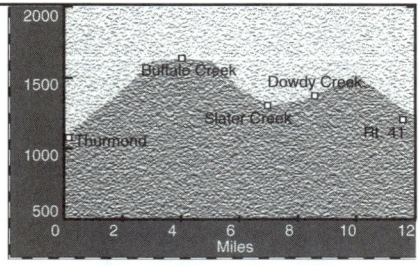

Length- 12 miles.
Difficulty- Moderate.
Elev. Change- 300 ft.
Points of Interest- Old town of Thurmond, Thayer, remote and scenic sections of Gorge.
Condition- Gravel road.

Trail Map- (p. 42)

How To Get There- The best starting point is at the Dunglen Day Use Area or the Stone Cliff River Access Area near Thurmond.

Description - At one time this road was bustling with activity from the mines and local people but now it is rarely used. It is a very scenic road that parallels the river for 12 miles. The road passes by abandoned coal mines and rustic Appalachian style houses. Mountain bikes are recommended on the rough road. The road is passable by most vehicles but cars with low ground clearance should avoid this road. The road crosses several mountain streams but water should not be consumed from these streams. There are no stores on this road to purchase drinks or food. The road ends on Route 41 near Prince.

Stone Cliff Trail

Length- 2.7 miles.
Difficulty- Moderate.
Elev. Change- 50 ft.
Points of Interest- Views of the New River and easy access to the river.
Condition- Old road bed. *Map* (p. 42)

How To Get There- From Dunglen continue following the dirt road about 1.5 miles upstream. Take a right on the gravel road just before crossing the bridge. The trailhead starts at the closed road beside the picnic area.

Description - Old road bed that follows the river for about 3 miles upstream. There is also a camping area at Stone Cliff and river access.

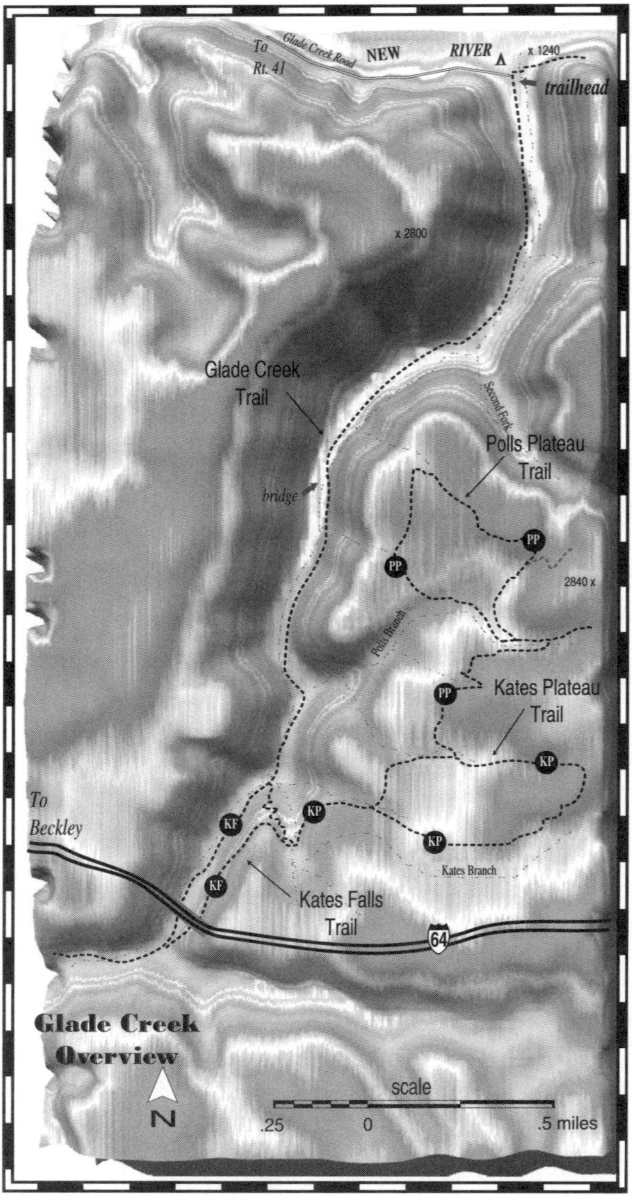

Map labels:

To Rt. 41 — Glade Creek Road — NEW RIVER ▲ x 1240 — *trailhead*

x 2800

Glade Creek Trail

Second Fork

Polls Plateau Trail

bridge — To

PP

PP

2840 x

Polls Branch

PP — Kates Plateau Trail

KP

To Beckley

KF — KP

KP

Kates Branch

KF — Kates Falls Trail — 64

Glade Creek Overview

N

scale
.25   0   .5 miles

Polls Plateau Loop Trail (PP)

Length- 4.1 miles.

Difficulty- Moderate.

Points of Interest- Remote wooded plateau, old farmlands.

Condition- Not Maintained.

Trailhead and Description- Starts off Kates Plateau Trail which is accessed from Glade Creek Trail and Kates Falls Trail.

Glade Creek Trail

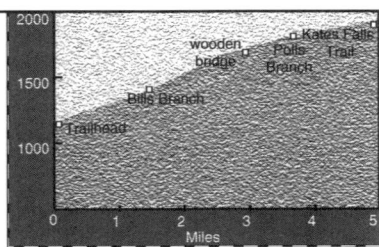

Length- 5.5 miles.
Difficulty- Moderate.
Elev. Change- 650 ft.
Points of Interest- Remote forest, wildlife, waterfall, and fishing.
Condition- Maintained.
Connections- Kates Falls Trail (4.6 miles).

Trail Map- (p. 44, 45)

Trailhead and Description- Trailhead is located at the end of the Glade Creek Access Road off Rt. 41. From the Rt. 41 turnoff it is a 5 mile drive on a gravel road to the trailhead. This is an excellent hiking trail in one of the most beautiful sections of the Gorge. Glade Creek is also stocked with trout and is popular with fishermen. It is 3 miles to the foot bridge.

Kates Falls Trail (KF)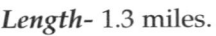

Length- 1.3 miles.
Difficulty- Hard.
Points of Interest- Kates Falls, views of Glade Creek Drainage.
Condition- Not Maintained.
Trailhead and Description- Trail begins and ends on Glade Creek Trail. From the Glade Creek Parking Area hike up Glade Creek Trail 4.6 miles to the Kates Falls Trail intersection.

Kates Plateau Trail (KP)

Length- 2.5 miles.
Difficulty- Moderate.
Points of Interest- Wooded plateau.
Condition- Not Maintained.
Trailhead and Description- Access is from the Kates Falls Trail. Hike Glade Creek Trail 4.6 to Kates Falls Trail intersection. This trail follows an old logging road through wooded plateau near wetlands.

Glade Creek profile looking upstream. Trailhead is at the bottom of the map.

Grandview

There are approximately seven miles of hiking trails in the Grandview area. Excellent scenic views of the New River Gorge, picnic facilities with shelters and easy hiking trails make this a great place for a days outing. Mountain biking is not allowed on trails but the Turkey Spur Road makes an enjoyable bike ride on a paved road.

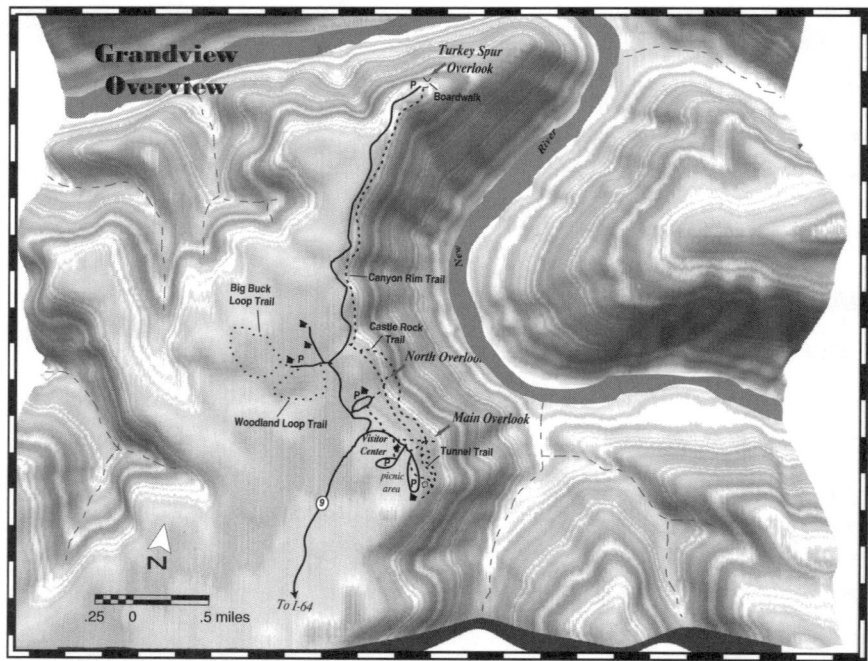

Grandview Overview. The New River flows from the right to the left.

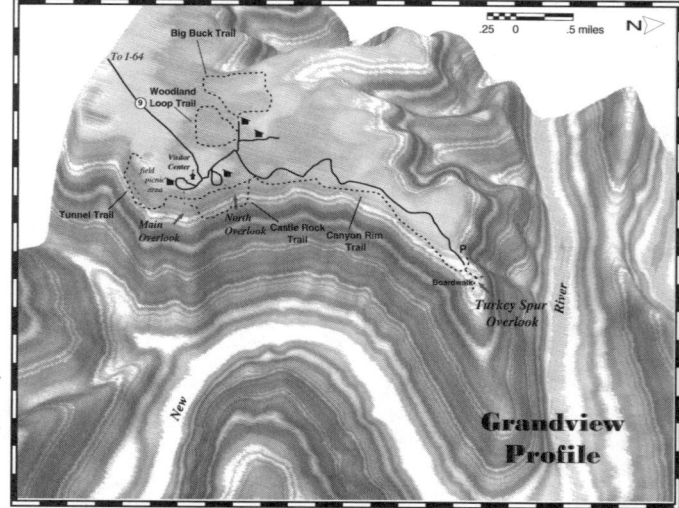

Grandview profile. The New River flows left to right.

Big Buck Loop Trail

Length- 0.7 miles RT.
Difficulty- Easy.
Points of Interest- Mature forest.
Condition- Maintained.
Trailhead and Description- Trailhead is located at shelter #6.

Canyon Rim Trail

Length- 1.6 miles OW.
Difficulty- Easy.
Points of Interest- Scenic overlooks of the New River and mature forests.
Condition- Maintained.
Trailhead and Description- Begin near the main overlook or the Turkey Spur Overlook. The trail follows the canyon rim offering excellent views of the gorge.

Castle Rock Trail

Length- 0.55 miles OW.
Difficulty- Moderate with exposed sections and stone steps.
Points of Interest- Scenic overlooks of the New River, rock formations.
Condition- Maintained.
Trailhead and Description- Trail begins near the main overlook parking area and connects with the Canyon Rim Trail. Trail follows base of cliff passing through interesting rock formations and boulders. Use caution on this trail.

Tunnel Trail

Length- 0.4 miles OW.
Difficulty- Easy.
Points of Interest- Tunnels and forest. Some tunnels may be closed.
Condition- Maintained.
Trailhead and Description- Trail begins near main overlook parking area or the ball field. Pass through tunnels and small caves along cliff and nice forest.

Turkey Spur Overlook

Length- .1 miles RT.
Difficulty- Easy.
Points of Interest- Overlook of New River.
Condition- Maintained.
Trailhead and Description- 150 steps up to scenic overlooks.

Woodland Loop Trail (Previous page/Grandview)

Length- 0.6 miles RT.
Difficulty- Easy.
Points of Interest- Open forest.
Condition- Maintained.
Trailhead and Description- Begin at picnic shelter #2.

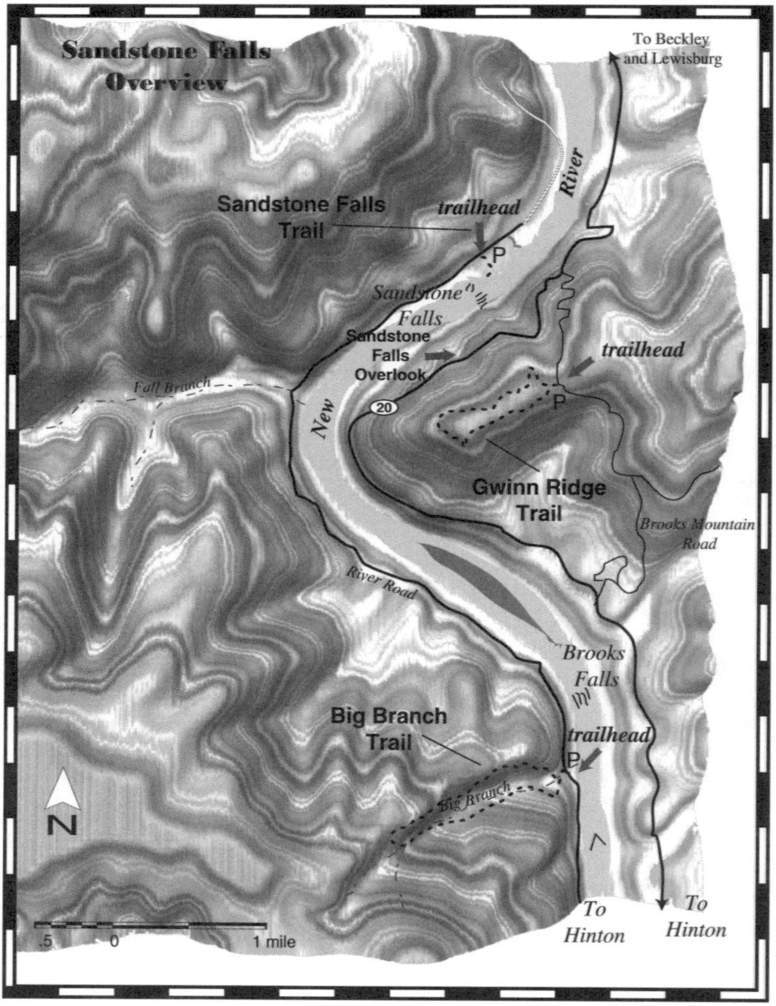

Sandstone Falls
Overview

To Beckley
and Lewisburg

River

Sandstone Falls
Trail

trailhead

P

Sandstone
Falls

Sandstone
Falls
Overlook

trailhead

Fall Branch

New

20

P

Gwinn Ridge
Trail

Brooks Mountain
Road

River Road

Brooks
Falls

Big Branch
Trail

trailhead

P

Big Branch

N

.5   0   1 mile

To
Hinton

To
Hinton

Sandstone Falls Loop Trail

Length- 0.5 miles.
Difficulty- Easy.
Points of Interest- Overlooks of Sandstone Falls.
Condition- Maintained.

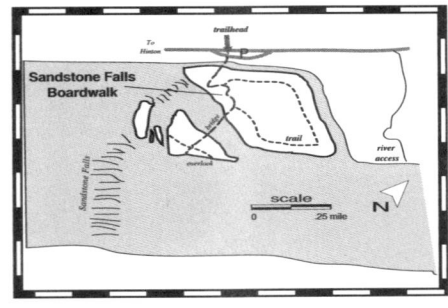

Trailhead and Description- Trail begins at Sandstone Falls Parking on River Road. Follow the board-walk as it passes through cedars and Virginia Pines. There is also a short trail that leads off the boardwalk, passes through a forest and then loops back to the boardwalk.

Big Branch Loop Trail

Length- 1.9 miles RT.
Difficulty- Moderate.
Points of Interest- 30 foot waterfall and mature forest.
Condition- Maintained. *Map* (p. 48)

Trailhead and Description- Trail starts across the road from the Brooks Falls Day Use Area. The trail follows Big Branch Creek passing by a 30 foot wa-terfall.

Gwinn Ridge Trail

Length- 3.5 miles RT.
Difficulty- Moderate.
Points of Interest- Ridge hike with nice views
Condition- Maintained. *Map* (p. 48)

Boardwalk at Sandstone Falls

Trailhead and Description- Follow Brooks Mountain Road about 2.5 miles up to the gap in the ridge near the Three Rivers Avian Center (bird reha-bilitation center). The trail follows an abandoned road along the ridge. The first part of the trail skirts the edge of the forest. The trail then drops down and contours through the forest offering nice views of the surround-ing area. The trail then regains the ridge and returns to the trailhead.

View of the New River from Grandview.

Rafters at Fayette Station.

Chapter 2

Babcock State Park · Hawk's Nest · Carnifex Ferry Battlefield

These three parks are located in close proximity to the New River. Babcock lies on the northern rim of the Gorge just opposite of Cunard. Hawk's Nest is also located on the northern rim of the Gorge and is the most downstream area covered in this book. Hawk's Nest is a small park with only a few miles of trails offering excellent views of the New River. Carnifex Ferry State Park is located on the Gauley River and is of historical importance because of a battle that was fought there during the Civil War. Babcock State Park covers about 4000 acres and has over twenty miles of trails for hiking and biking. Babcock has campgrounds and cabins for visitors and Hawk's Nest maintains lodge facilities for visitors.

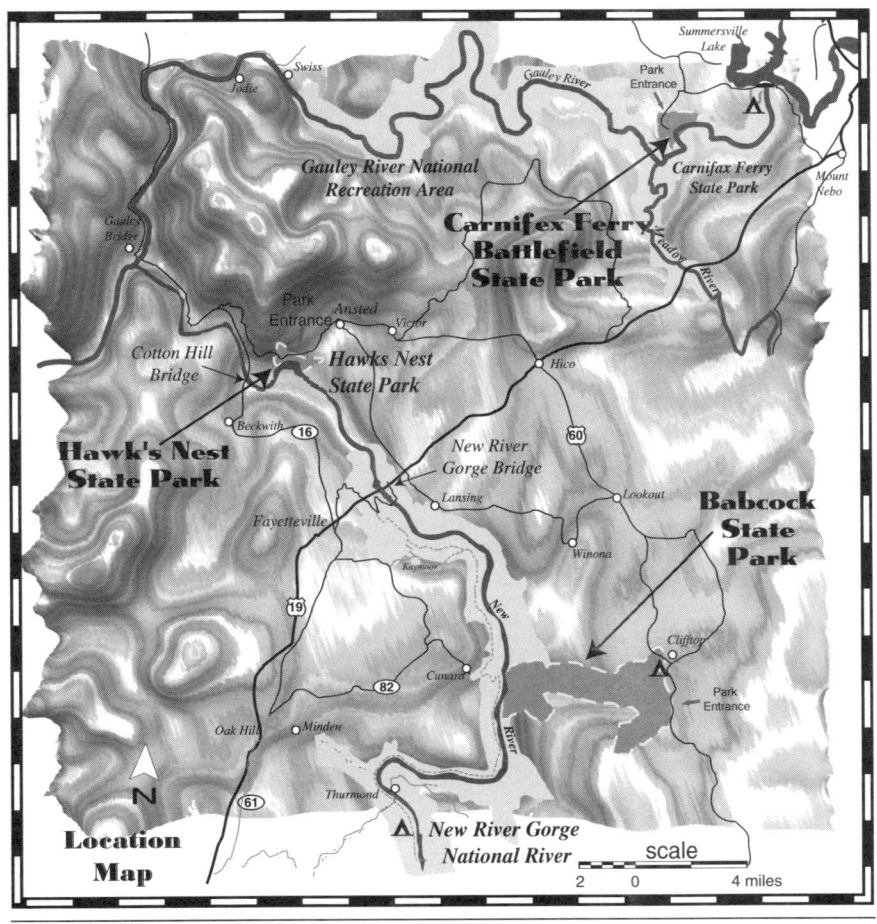

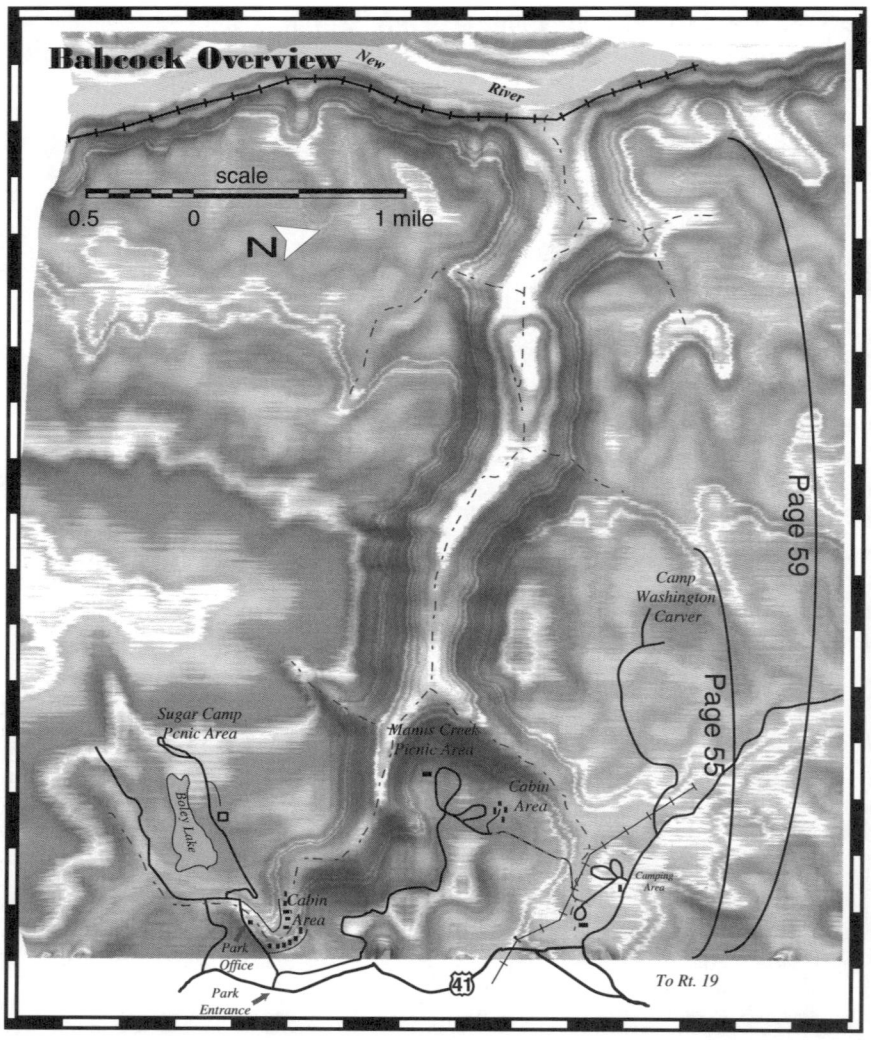

Babcock Overview

New River

scale

0.5   0   1 mile

N

Page 59

Page 55

Camp Washington Carver

Sugar Camp Penic Area

Manns Creek Picnic Area

Boley Lake

Cabin Area

Cabin Area

Camping Area

Park Office

Park Entrance

41

To Rt. 19

Babcock State Park

Babcock State Park is one of the hidden treasures of West Virginia. Roughly 4000 acres of lush forest, waterfalls, boulder-strewn streams, and rugged terrain will give you a taste of rustic West Virginia. The Park is situated in a large canyon which is drained by Glade Creek and Mann's Creek. Both of these creeks empty into the New River. The canyon contains 20+ miles of hiking trails. There is also a riding stable, swimming pool, small lake and boat rentals, tennis courts, volleyball courts and other recreational activities. Excellent camping and cabin facilities are also available on a seasonal bases. The park is open from mid-April to October 31.

For more information contact:

Babcock State Park
HC 35, Box 150
Clifftop, West Virginia 25831
tel. (304) 438-3004

Cliffline along the top of the New River Gorge.

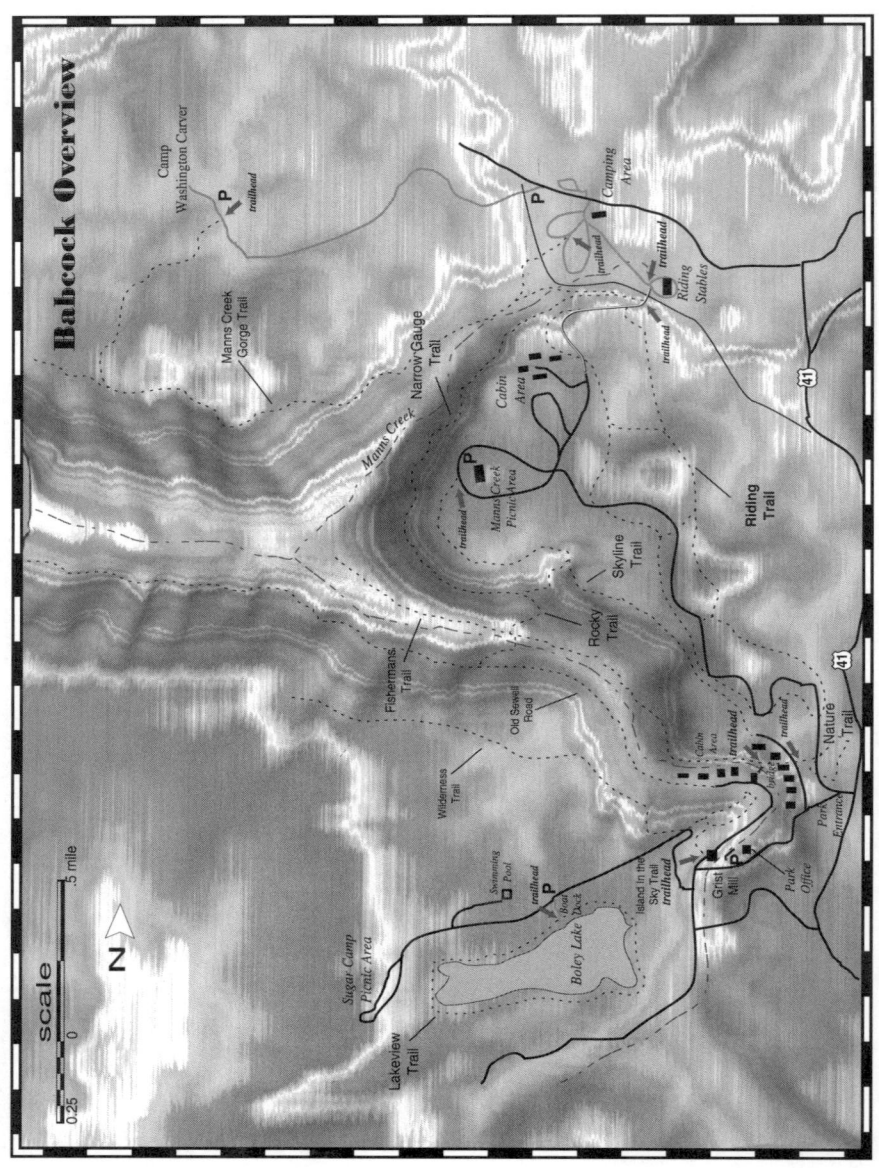

Babcock Overview

scale

0.25   0   .5 mile

N

Lakeview Trail

Sugar Camp Picnic Area

Swimming Pool

trailhead   P

Boley Lake

Island in the Sky Trail trailhead

Wilderness Trail

Fishermans Trail

Old Sewell Road

Rocky Trail

Skyline Trail

Manns Creek Picnic Area

trailhead   P

Cabin Area

Narrow-Gauge Trail

Manns Creek

Manns Creek Gorge Trail

Camp Washington Carver

P   trailhead

Camping Area

P   trailhead

trailhead   Riding Stables

Riding Trail

41

Nature Trail

41

Cabin Area   trailhead   trailhead

Grist Mill   P

Park Office

Park Entrance

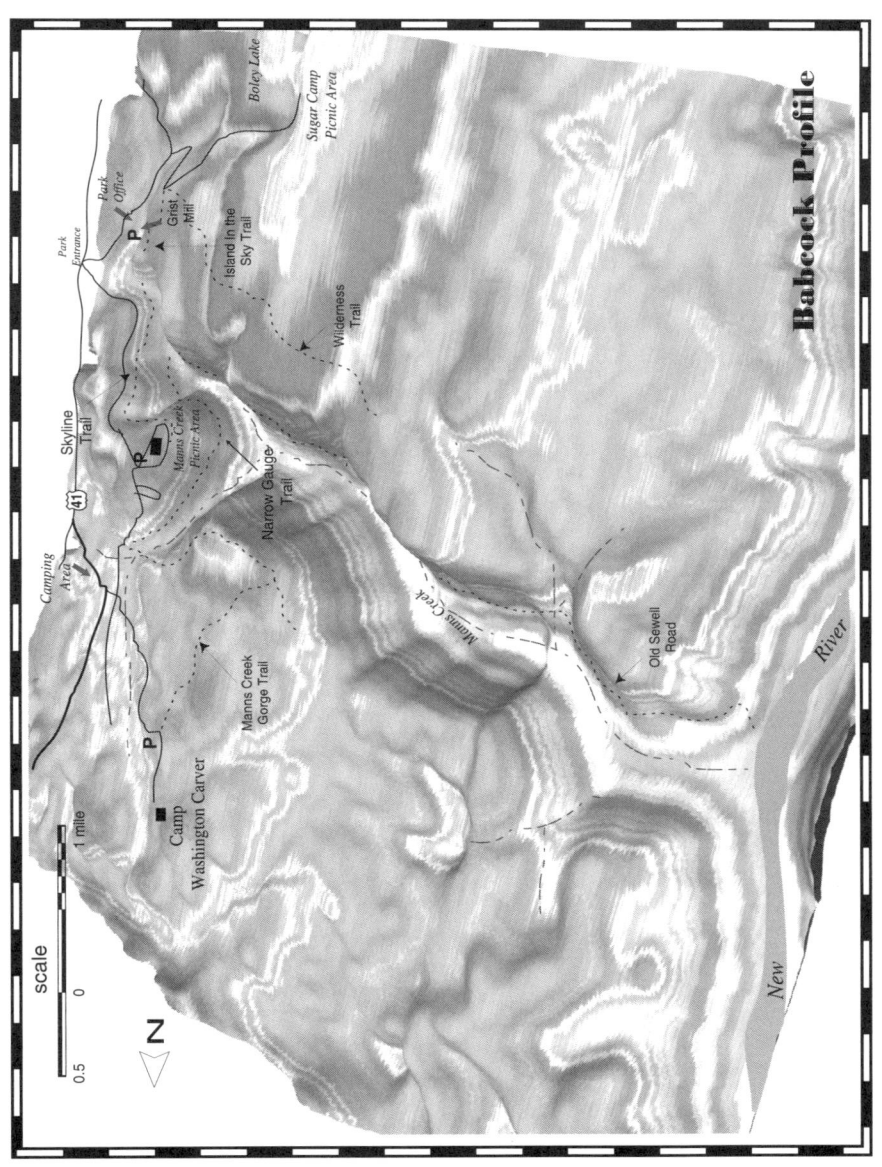

Babcock Profile

scale

0.5   0   1 mile

N

Camping Area

Skyline Trail

(41)

Camp Washington Carver

Manns Creek Gorge Trail

Narrow Gauge Trail

Manns Creek Picnic Area

Park Entrance

Park Office

Grist Mill

Island in the Sky Trail

Wilderness Trail

Boley Lake

Sugar Camp Picnic Area

Manns Creek

Old Sewell Road

New River

Fisherman's Trail

Length- 2.2 miles RT.
Difficulty- Moderate.
Elev. Change- 500 ft.
Condition- Maintained but rugged.
Trailhead and Description-

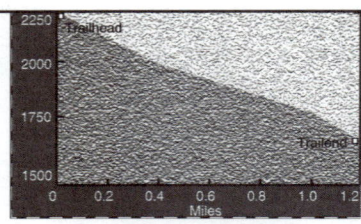

Trail Map- (p. 54)

The trailhead is located along Glade Creek at the north end of the bridge between cabins 7 and 5. The trail follows Glade Creek down to the intersection of Glade and Manns Creek. It is also possible to linkup with Rocky Trail approximately half way down the trail.

Island in the Sky

Length- 0.2 miles OW.
Difficulty- Easy.
Elev. Change- 110 ft.
Points of Interest- Scenic views of the park and old Grist Mill.
Condition- Maintained.
Trailhead and Description- Trailhead is

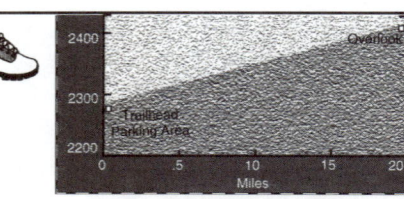

Trail Map- (p. 54)

located at the Gristmill near the Administration Building. Follow the trail as it ascends to the top of the cliff and overlook opposite the Administration building.

Lake View Loop Trail

Length- 1 mile RT.
Difficulty- Easy.
Elev. Change- 30 ft.
Points of Interest- Active beaver population.
Condition- Maintained.

Trail Map- (p. 54)

Trailhead and Description- Trailhead is located at the boat dock. Follow the trail as it circles the lake.

Narrow Gauge Trail

Length- 1.5 miles OW.
Difficulty- Easy.
Points of Interest- Scenic forest.
Condition- Maintained.

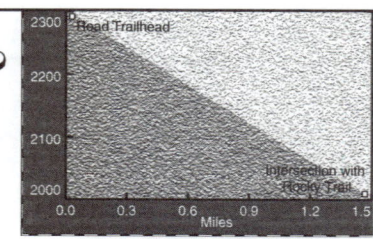

Trail Map- (p. 54)

Trailhead and Description- This trail contours around the point between Manns Creek and Glade Creek. Excellent trail

Riding Trail Loop

Length- 3.5 miles RT.
Difficulty- Easy.
Elev. Change- 200 ft.
Points of Interest- Scenic forest.
Condition- Maintained.
Trailhead and Description- Start at the

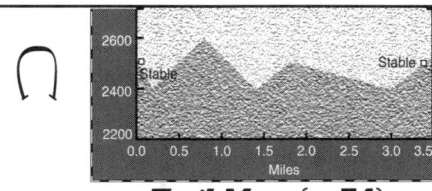

Trail Map- (p. 54)

riding stables and make a complete loop passing through scenic woodlands.

Rocky Trail

Length- 1.2 mile OW.
Difficulty- Easy.
Elev. Change- 270 ft.
Points of Interest- Scenic views.
Condition- Maintained.
Trailhead and Description- Access to this

Trail Map- (p. 54)

trail is either from the Fisherman's Trail or from Skyline Trail.

Skyline Trail

Length- 1.5 miles OW.
Difficulty- Easy.
Elev. Change- 270 ft.
Points of Interest- Spectacular
views and overlooks of park.
Condition- Maintained.

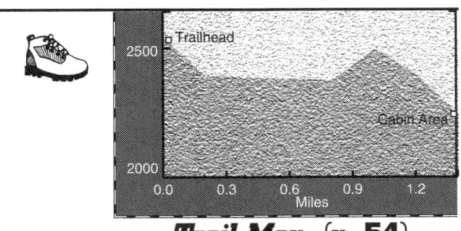

Trail Map- (p. 54)

Trailhead and Description- Trailhead is
located across the road from cabins 4 and 5 in the Cabin Area or the Manns
Creek picnic area. This trail follows the top of the cliffline of Glade Creek
Canyon allowing for excellent scenic views of the park. It is also possible
to linkup with Rocky Trail from Skyline Trail.

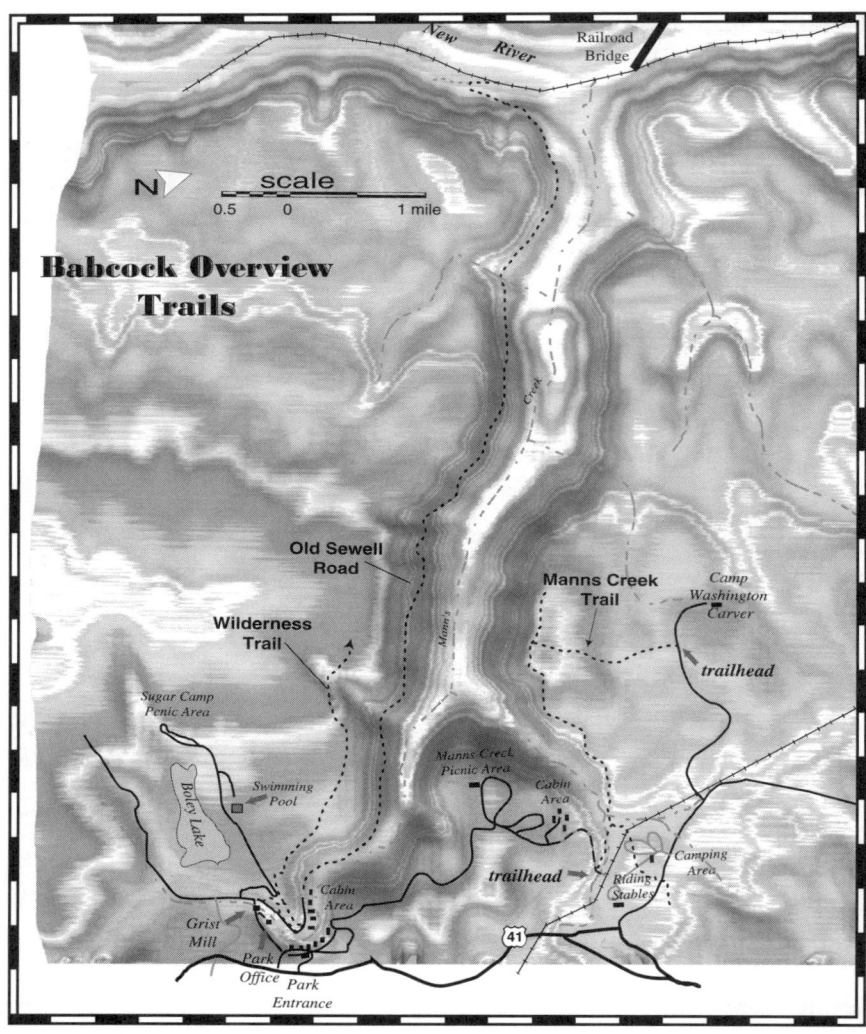

Babcock Overview Trails

New River
Railroad Bridge

N
scale
0.5 0 1 mile

Old Sewell Road

Wilderness Trail

Manns Creek Trail

Camp Washington Carver

trailhead

Sugar Camp Penic Area

Manns Creek

Manns Creek Picnic Area

Cabin Area

Camping Area

Boley Lake

Swimming Pool

trailhead

Riding Stables

Cabin Area

Grist Mill

Park Office

Park Entrance

41

Manns Creek Trail

Length- 2 miles OW.
Difficulty- Moderate.
Elev. Change- 300 ft.
Points of Interest- Excellent views of Manns Creek Canyon and abundant spring wildflowers.
Condition- Maintained.

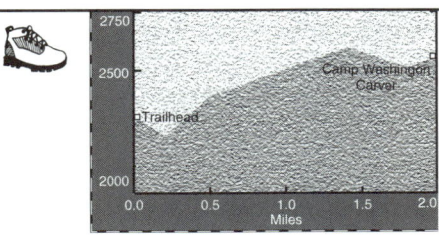

Trail Map- (p. 58)

Trailhead and Description- Trailhead is located in the campground area across from campsite #26 or the trailhead is located at Camp Washington Carver.

Old Sewell Road

Length- 5.2 miles OW.
Difficulty- Moderate.
Elev. Change- 1250 ft.
Points of Interest- Manns Creek Gorge.
Condition- Maintained.

Trailhead and Description- Follow road past Grist Mill on western side of Manns Creek until the pavement ends. Continue following dirt road down Manns Creek Canyon to New River.

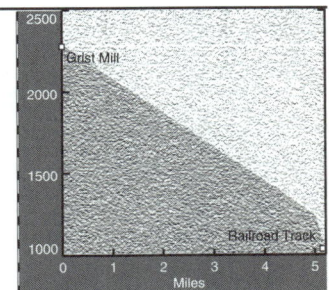

Trail Map- (p. 58)

Wilderness Trail

Length- 2.5+ miles OW.
Difficulty- Moderate.
Elev. Change- 130 ft.
Points of Interest- Remote area.
Condition- Maintained.

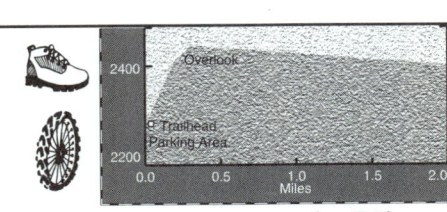

Trail Map- (p. 58)

Trailhead and Description- Trail starts at the second sharp turn on the road to the lake and follows canyon rim. Remote hiking in wilderness setting.

Hawk's Nest

Hawk's Nest State Park is located near the small town of Anstead. This park sits on the rim of the New River Gorge and offers scenic views of the canyon and river. From Anstead follow Rt. 60 west.

For more information contact: **Hawk's Nest State Park**
Ansted, WV
(304) 658-5196.

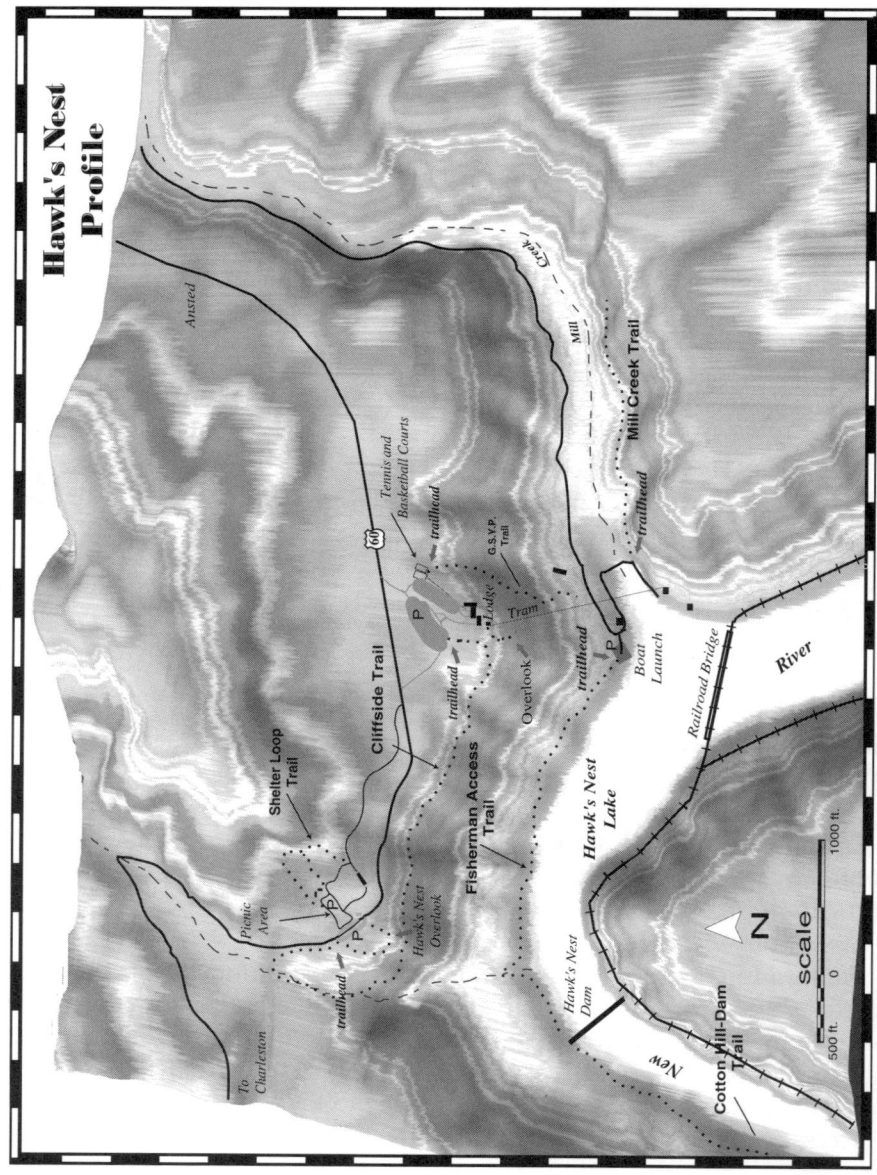

Cliffside Trail

Length- 1.75 miles OW.
Difficulty- Easy.
Points of Interest- Turkey Creek falls, rock formations.
Condition- Maintained.
Trailhead and Description- Trailhead is located at the Midland Trail Shelter near the main lodge or the parking area at Hawk's Nest Overlook. From the shelter, trail drops down to the cliff and follows the cliff base then passes through scenic wooded area.

Fishermen's Access Trail

Length- 0.5 mile OW.
Difficulty- Easy.
Points of Interest- View of dam.
Condition- Maintained.
Trailhead and Description- Trail starts at western end of the river parking area near the boat launch. Trail follows the north edge of Hawk's Nest Lake.

G.S.Y.P. Trail

Length- 0.75 mile OW.
Difficulty- Easy.
Condition- Maintained.
Trailhead and Description- Trail starts at tennis courts and descends to the New River passing through hardwood forests.

Loop Trail

Length- 0.5 mile RT.
Difficulty- Easy.
Condition- Maintained.
Trailhead and Description- Trail begins at picnic shelter and makes a loop through forest.

Cotton Hill to Hawk's Nest Dam Trail

Length- 1 mile OW.
Difficulty- Easy.
Condition- Maintained.
Trailhead and Description- This trail is not accessed from the Hawk's Nest area but downstream from the dam off Route 16. Park in the established parking area on the north side of the Cotton Hill bridge. A dam access road runs parallel to the river and has several side trails that drop down to the river. It is possible to hike all the way to the base of the dam on the access road.

Carnifex Ferry Battlefield State Park

Carnifex Ferry is located adjacent to the Gauley River and offers easy access to the river. The state park is of historical importance due to a civil war battle that was fought in the area on Sept. 10, 1861. Confederate troops led by General John B. Floyd were engaged and forced to retreat by troops led by Union General William Rosecrans. The confederate forces lost control of the Kanawha Valley and as a result West Virginia was able to declare statehood without threat from the confederate forces.

There are several short hiking trails plus picnic facilities at the park.

For more information contact:

Carnifex Ferry Battlefield State Park
Route 2 Box 435
Summersville, WV 26651
304-872-0825

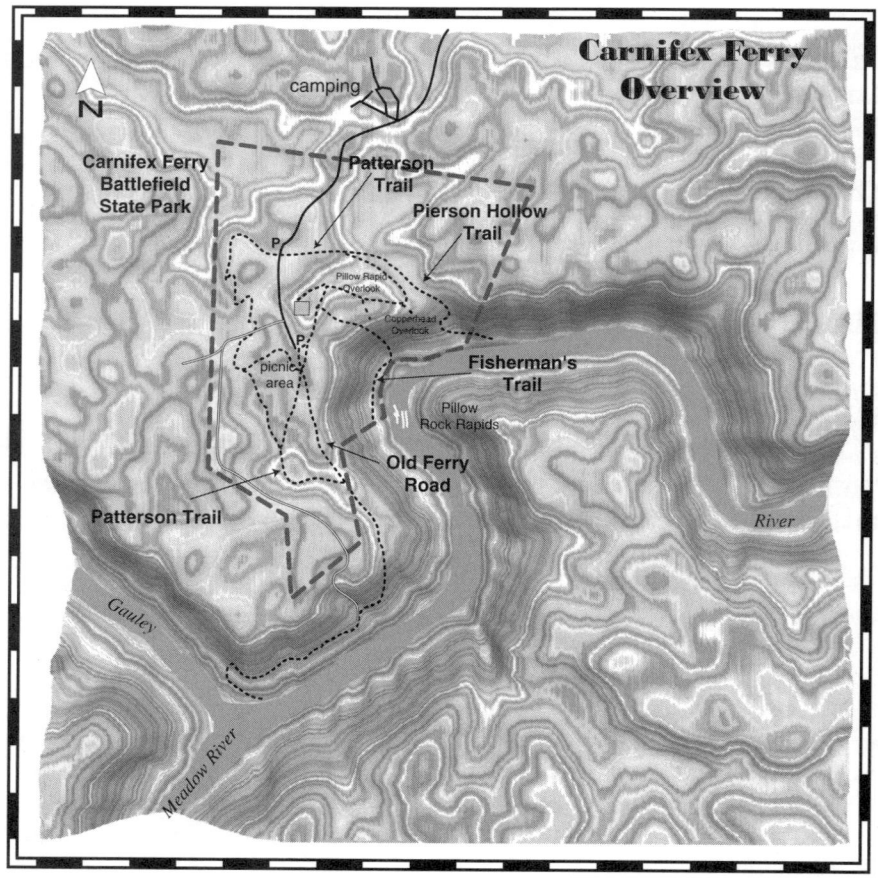

Old Carnifex Road

Length- 1.5 miles OW.
Difficulty- Moderate
Points of Interest- Retreat path used by Confederate General Floyd.
Condition- Maintained.
Trailhead and Description- Begins at picnic shelter #3 and ends at the site of the old ferry that crossed the Gauley River.

Fisherman's Trail

Length- .6 miles OW.
Difficulty- Difficult.
Points of Interest- Access to river.
Condition- Maintained.
Trailhead and Description- Begins at the main overlook near the parking area. Steep and fairly strenuous hike down to the river. Great place to access the Pillow Rock rapid area.

Patterson Trail

Length- 2 miles OW.
Difficulty- Moderate
Points of Interest- Overlooks of the Gauley River.
Condition- Maintained.
Trailhead and Description- This trail may be accessed from several points. It forms a loop around the park.

Pierson Hollow Trail

Length- .8 miles OW.
Difficulty- Difficult.
Points of Interest- Access to the Gauley River
Condition- Maintained.
Trailhead and Description- Branches off the Patterson Trail and descends to the river on a steep and more strenuous trail.

Mountain biker Dan Foster crossing one of the old railroad trestles.

Chapter 3

Greenbrier River Trail · Cranberry Glades Wilderness Area

These two areas complement the New River Gorge area nicely. The Greenbrier Trail offers a beautiful and extended trail for multiple day biking or hiking. The Cranberry offers remote wilderness settings for extended backpacking, biking and cross-country skiing. From Fayetteville, the Cranberry Wilderness Area may be reached in one hour and fifteen minutes. Lewisburg is also one and one-half hours from the Fayetteville area and approximately forty minutes from the Cranberry Area. Also nearby is the Greenbrier State Forest, Watoga State Park, Calvin Price State Forest, Seneca State Forest and a large area of the Monongahela National Forest. These areas have excellent hiking trails, camping areas and remote scenic forests but are not covered in this guidebook.

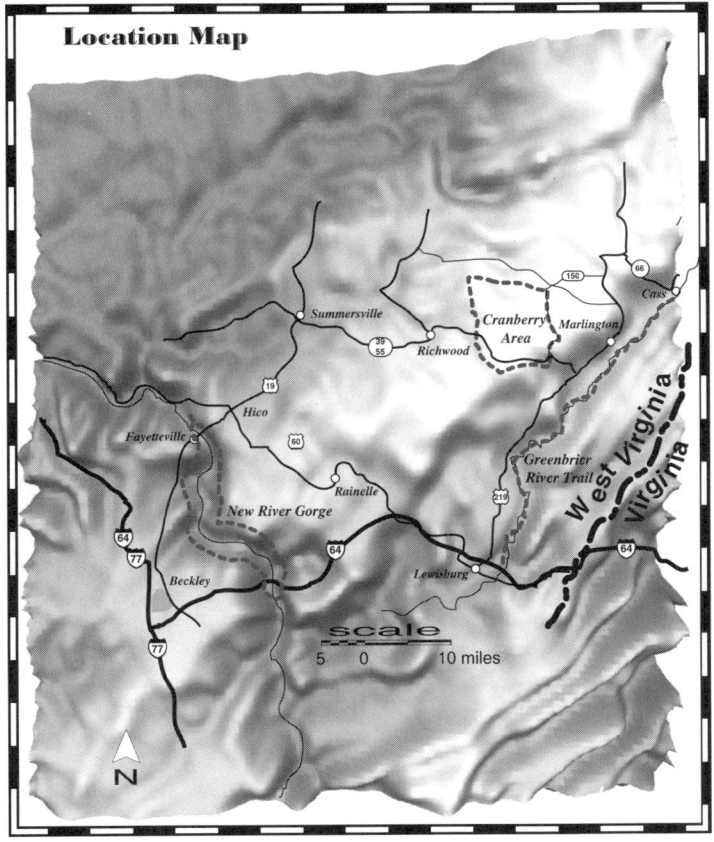

Rock climber high above the New River.

Old mill near Route 16.

Greenbrier River Trail

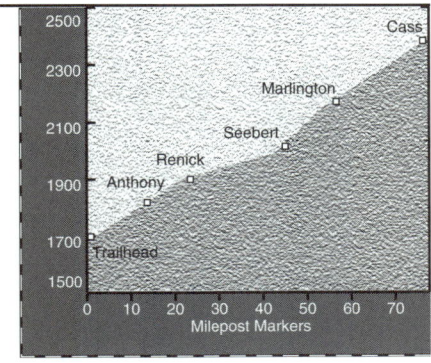

Length- 75 miles.
Difficulty- Easy to moderate.
Elev. Change- 600 ft.
Points of Interest- Scenic river, historical towns, remote forests.
Condition- Railroad bed varies from hard packed to gravel surface.

How To Get There- There are several access points to the Greenbrier Trail. Many of the small towns adjacent to the trail have easy access points (refer to map). The most popular starting point is either from North Caldwell at the southern end of the trail and Cass or Sitlington (for bikes) at the northern end. To reach the southern trailhead (North Caldwell) from Lewisburg, take US 60 east and turn left on to Stone House Road just west of the Greenbrier River bridge. Drive 1.4 miles north to the trailhead.

Trail Description- The Greenbrier River Trail is a railroad bed that has been converted to a hiking and biking trail. It is administered by the West Virginia State Park System. The trail runs adjacent to the Greenbrier River and maintains a fairly level gradient throughout with Cass upstream and Caldwell downstream. The trail passes through many small towns. The trail description in this book breaks the trail down in segments and lists available facilities on certain sections of trails. Most of these towns have basic supplies, telephone, and water. They also provide easy access to the trail. It is possible to start or finish at any of these access points on the trail for a combination of short day trips or longer multiple day trips.

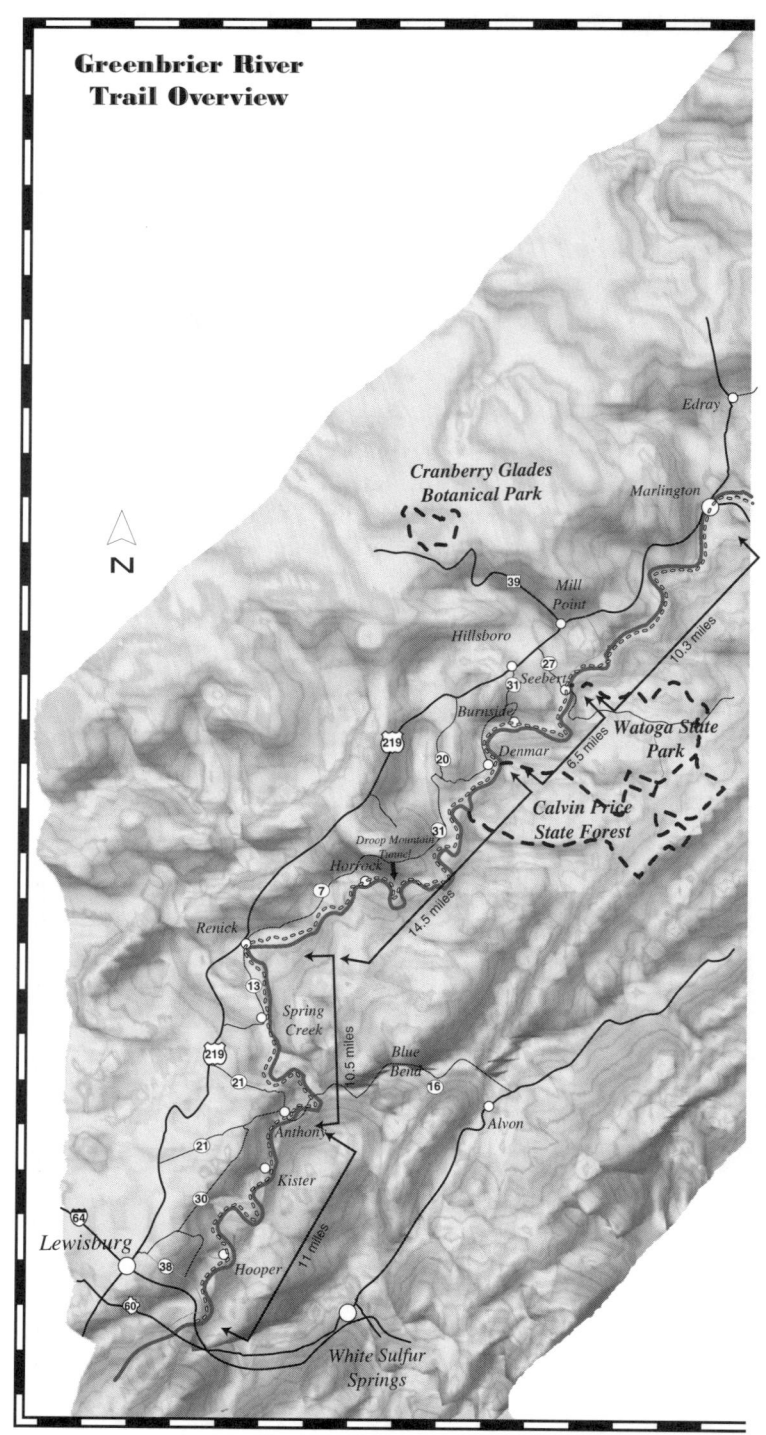

Greenbrier River Trail Overview

Edray

Cranberry Glades
Botanical Park

Marlington

N

Mill Point

39

Hillsboro

27

Seebert

31

Burnside

219

20

Denmar

Watoga State
Park

10.3 miles

6.5 miles

Calvin Price
State Forest

Droop Mountain
Tunnel

31

Horrock

7

14.5 miles

Renick

13

Spring
Creek

Blue
Bend

219

16

21

10.5 miles

Alvon

21

Anthony

Kister

30

11 miles

Lewisburg

64

38

Hooper

60

White Sulfur
Springs

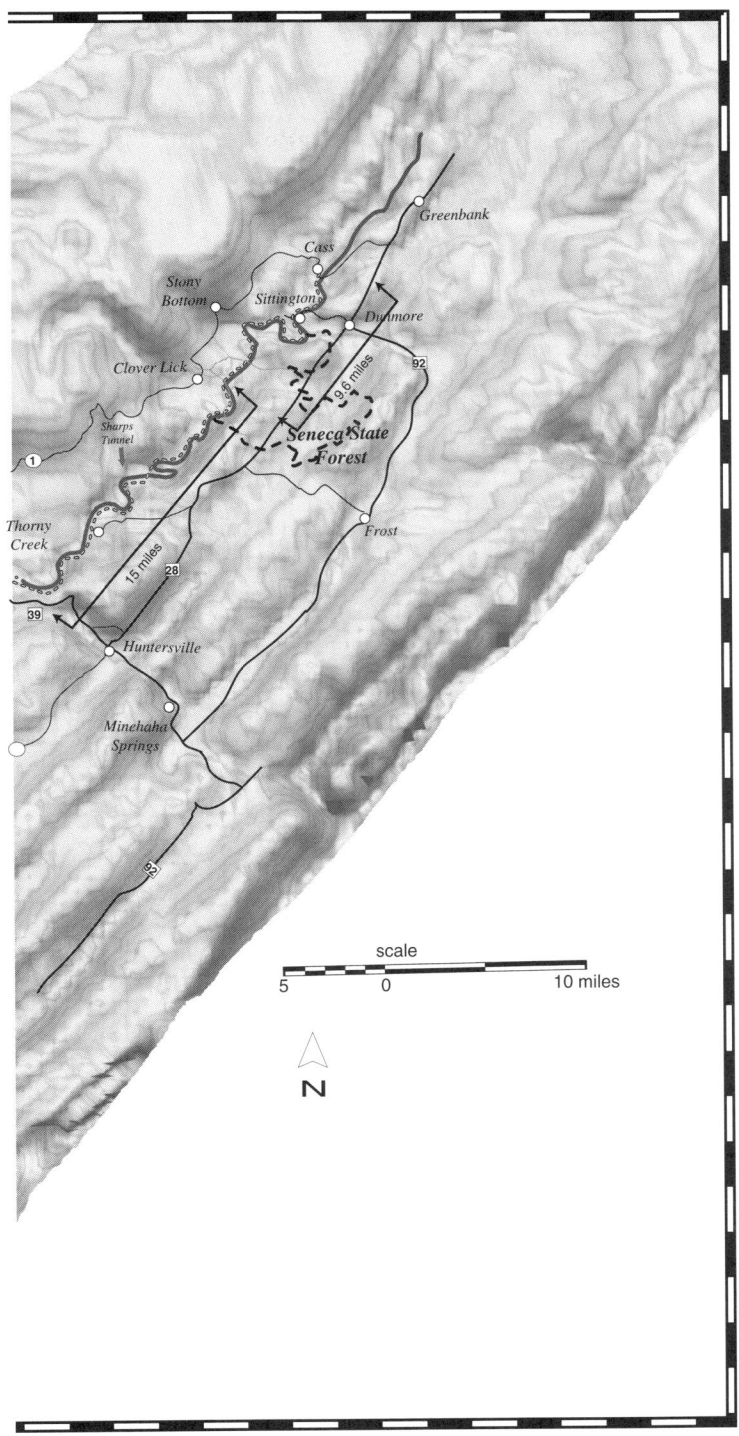

Greenbank

Cass

Stony
Bottom
Sittington

Clover Lick
Dunmore

92

9.6 miles

Sharps
Tunnel

Seneca State
Forest

1

Frost

Thorny
Creek

15 miles
28

39

Huntersville

Minehaha
Springs

scale

5   0   10 miles

N

Greenbrier River Trail Description

Milage	Access/Camping	Description
0	**North Caldwell.** Groceries, phone, water and camping area 2 miles east of Caldwell on US **60 in Greenbrier State Forest.**	High scenic value and fairly remote.
3	**Trailhead. Trail access. Located approximately 1.4 miles north of Caldwell and US 60 on Co. Rt. 38.**	
4.7	**Campsite. No facilities.**	
5.8	**Hopper.**	
11	**Keister.**	
13.5	**Campsite.** No facilities.	
14	**Anthony.** Trail access point with phone and food in Frankfort. Campsites located across bridge on Anthony Creek Trail and near river.	Trail continues on west side of river passing through scenic mountains and pastures.
16:	**Woodman.**	
21.5	**Spring Creek.**	
28.5	**Renick.** Trail access.	
29.6	**Horrock.** Trail access and parking.	Trail continues on west side of river passing through the Droop Mountain Tunnel.
31	**Droop Mountain Tunnel** (402 feet long). Campsite (east side of trail) and unapproved spring (west side of trail) just north of tunnel.	
32.2	**Campsite.** East side of trail, no facilities.	
33.7	**Campsite.** Spring on west side of trail and campsite on west side.	
38.5	**Beard.** Trail access, parking area and Bed & Breakfast.	
39.3	**Denmar** Trail access and parking. Location of State Hospital.	
40.9	**Campsite**. No facilities or water.	Trail continues on west side of river. Trail runs opposite Watoga State Park.
41.7	**Burnside.** Trail access and parking.	
44	**Camping.** Watoga State Park fee campground on east side of river. No bridge. Ford river or cross at Seebert.	
45.8	**Seebert.** Trail access and parking. Cross bridge to Watoga State Park. Campground and cabins with full facilities, phone, water and restaurant.	
47.9	Watoga Bridge. Trail access to east side of river.	

Milage	Access/Camping	Description
48.1	Watoga. Old town site.	Trail continues on west side of river crossing to the east side at the at the Watoga Bridge.
52.2	**Buckeye.** Trail access and parking.	
55.1	**Stillwell.** Camping area.	
56.1	**Marlington.** Trail access, food, water (restored train depot), phone, hospital (west of depot on Main Street) and lodging.	
56.5	**Water Tank.**	Trail continues on east side of river crossing to the west side at Sharp s Bridge. It then passes through Sharp s Tunnel. Perhaps the most scenic and remote section of the trail.
61.3	**Thorny Creek.**	
62.3	**Clawson.**	
63.7	**Campsite.** East side of trail	
65.7	**Sharp s Tunnel.** 511 feet long and built in 1900.	
69.6	**Campsite.** East side of trail.	
70.3	**Grease reservoir.** Remains of old greasing station for the wheel flanges on trains.	
71.1	**Clover Lick.** Trail access point and parking area.	Trail continues on west side of river. Bikers usually start or finish at the Sitlington access point. Tracks are still in place on sections between Cass and Sitlington.
74.4	**Stony Bottom.** Trail access, lodging and parking.	
77	**Sitlington.** Trail access. This is the recommended access point for bikes.	
80	**Cass.** Trail access, food, lodging and phone.	

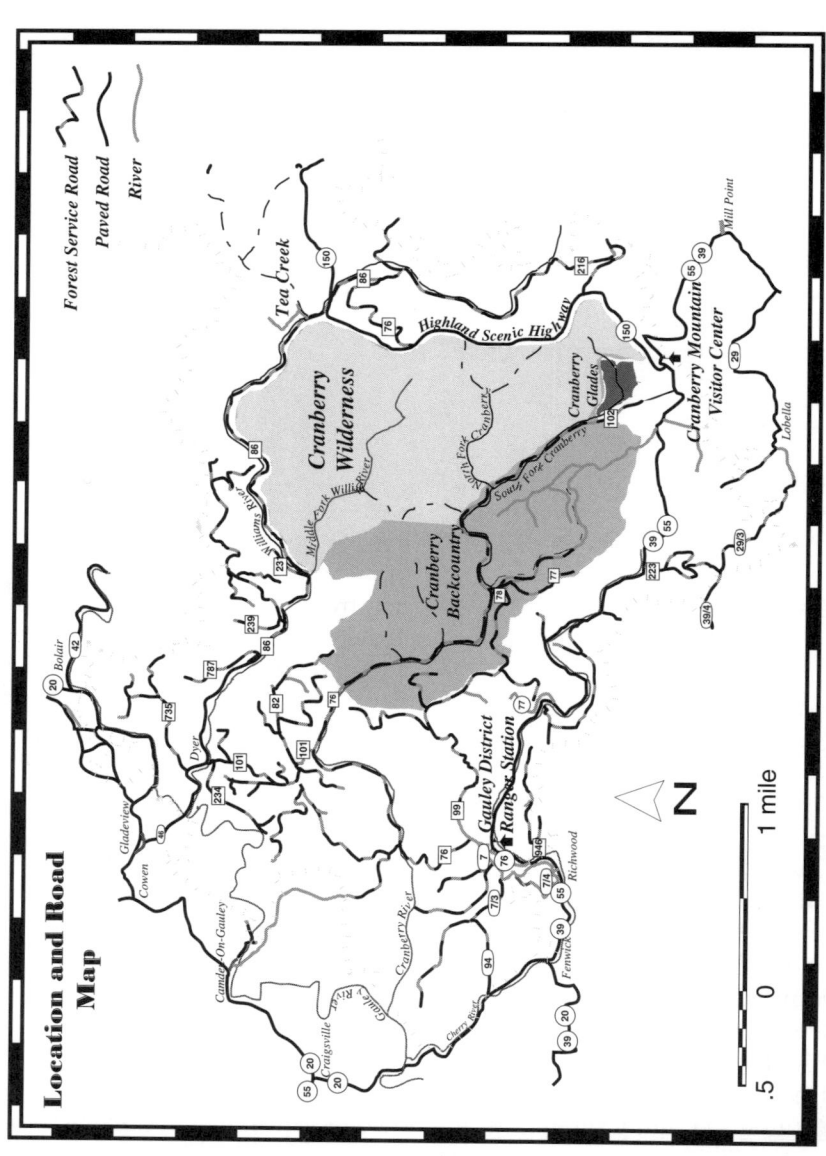

Location and Road Map

Forest Service Road
Paved Road
River

Cranberry Wilderness

Cranberry Backcountry

Cranberry Glades

Highland Scenic Highway

Tea Creek

Middle Fork Williams River

Williams River

North Fork Cranberry

South Fork Cranberry

Cranberry Mountain Visitor Center

Mill Point

Lobelia

Gauley District Ranger Station

Richwood

Fenwick

Camden-On-Gauley

Cranberry River

Gauley River

Gladeview

Cowen

Dyer

Craigsville

Cherry River

Blair

N

.5   0   1 mile

Cranberry Wilderness Area

The Cranberry Wilderness Area was designated Wilderness Area in 1983 by the Wilderness Act of 1964, one of the best pieces of legislation passed by our legislation. As a wilderness area, all forms of exploitation are illegal (mining, timbering, road building, construction, etc..). Vehicles are also prohibited. The 35,864 acre forest is one of the true wilderness areas in West Virginia. Please respect this while backpacking or hiking. Immediately to the west of the Wilderness Area is the Cranberry Back Country. The Back Country has similar restrictions to the Wilderness Area but it is slightly smaller and consists of 26,000 acres of land. Logging is permitted in the Back Country as well as Forest Service vehicles and mountain bikes. There is a network of roads in the Back Country Area closed to motor vehicle traffic. These roads are excellent for mountain biking. The Wilderness Area contains about 60 miles of hiking trail and the Back Country contains about 75 miles of trail. Permits are not required for the Back Country or the Wilderness Area. If you plan on backpacking or hiking in the area leave your trip itinerary with friends or family in case of an emergency.

Weather
The Cranberry Area ranges in elevation from 3000 to 4600 feet. Temperatures in the summer range from 70-80 degrees Fahrenheit and in the winter it can drop to -25 degrees. The area receives about 60 inches of rain annually and 90 inches of snow. Always be prepared for the worst! For extended trips or even day trips bring adequate clothing. Even in the summer, it is possible to become hypothermic if you are wearing only cotton clothing and get caught in the wind and rain on a ridge.

Camping Areas
There are four developed fee camping areas. Campgrounds have water and toilet facilities. Sites are furnished with picnic tables, parking space and fireplaces. Electricity and firewood are not provided.
Summit Lake- 10 miles east of Richwood on Rt. 39/55. Open March 15-Dec. 1. Daily fee is $5.
Big Rock- 6 miles north on Forest Road 76 north of Rt. 39/55. March 15-Dec.1. Daily fee $5 to $8.
Cranberry Campground- Located on Forest Road 76 about 7 miles northeast of Big Rock Campground. Sites range from $5 to $8 a day.
Bishop Knob- Located on Forest Road 101. Access from Big Rock Campground or from Rt. 46. Open April 1 to Dec.1. Daily fee $2.

Water

Water in streams and rivers should not be considered safe to consume unless it has been boiled, filtered or treated for organisms such as Giardia.

Trails

The trail system in the Cranberry Area is extensive and open year round. In general, trails either follow a stream or river system or follow the tops of ridges. Hiking is permitted on all of the trails while mountain bikes are prohibited in the Cranberry Wilderness Area. Due to the high elevation, the area receives a large amount of snowfall during the winter months and many of the trails are excellent cross country ski trails. Most of the United States Forest Service trails are marked with blue blazes or blue plastic diamonds. Trails vary from old logging roads to rugged single track trails. The maps used in this guide are not highly detailed. For full detail maps, use USGS topographic maps. Always bring a compass in the event you become disoriented.

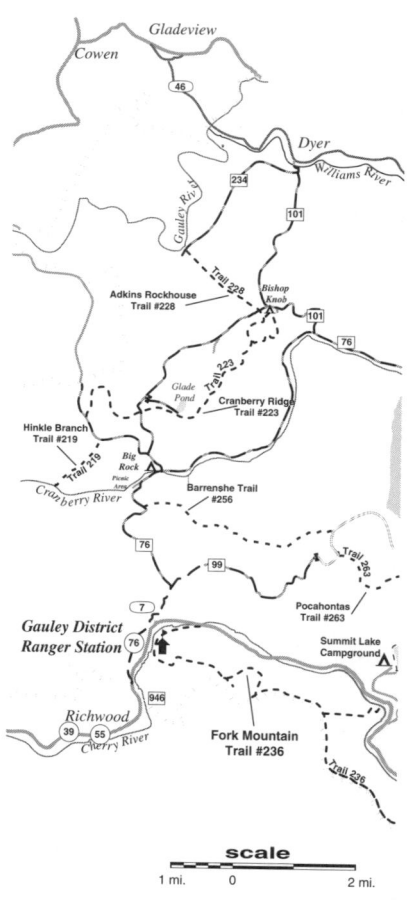

Shelters

Seven shelters are located along Forest Road 102 and 76. These are small wooden structures with three walls that hold 6 to 10 people each. They cannot be reserved and are available to anyone on a first-come basis.

Hazards

The only threat from poisonous animals comes from copperheads and rattle snakes. Be familiar with identifying these snakes and if you stumble across one stay out of its way. Remember that you are the visitor and this is their home. Mosquitoes and black flies are common in some areas. Poison Ivy is also common on trails. Be familiar with this plant. If you are lucky, you may see a black bear. They are timid creatures and rarely observed. The area is a designated black bear sanctuary. Hunting and Fishing is permitted throughout the Cranberry

---

Back Country and Cranberry Wilderness Areas. A National Forest Stamp, Conservation Stamp, Trout Stamp, and state hunting and fishing licenses are required. The main hunting season runs from about mid-November to December. Avoid hiking or being in the forest during hunting season or at least wear bright orange or red.

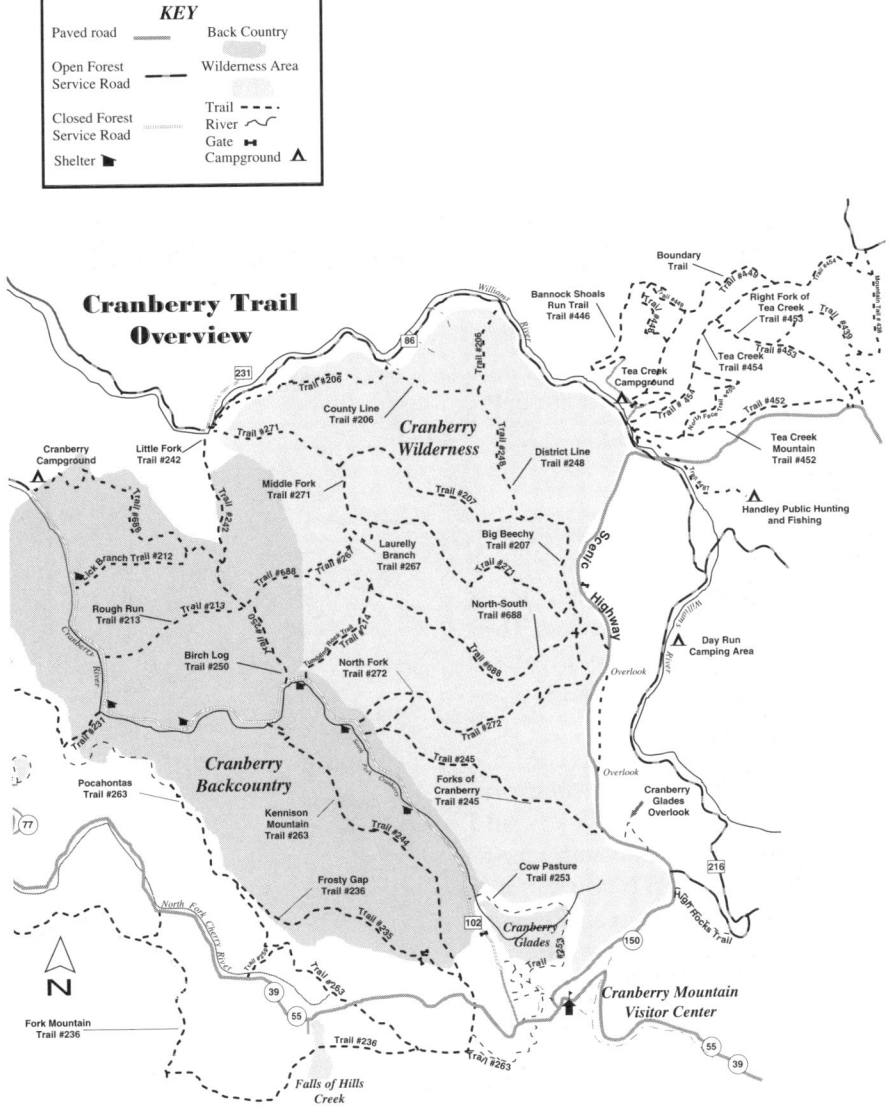

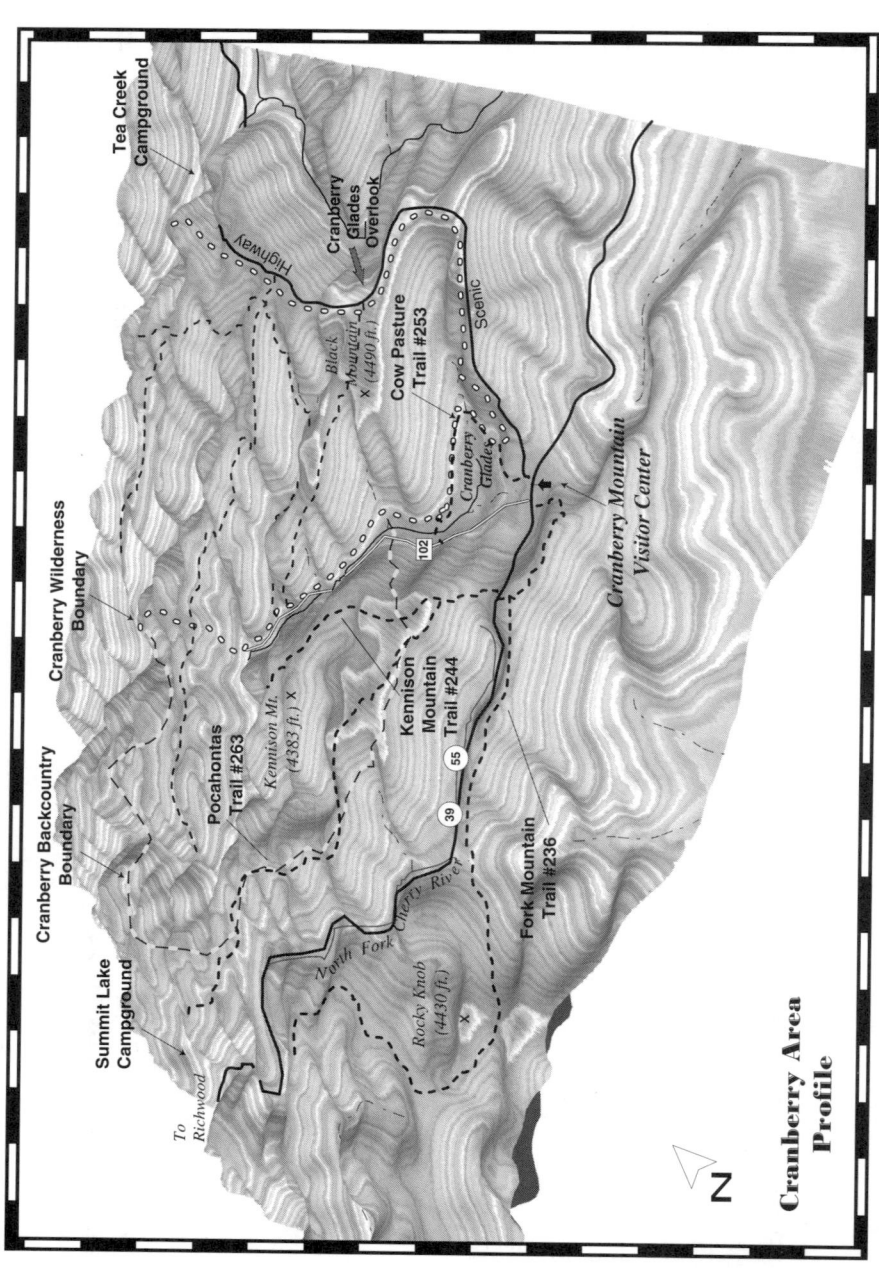

Tea Creek Campground

Cranberry Glades Overlook

Highway

Black Mountain X (4490 ft.)

Cow Pasture Trail #253

Scenic

Cranberry Glades

Cranberry Wilderness Boundary

102

Cranberry Mountain Visitor Center

Cranberry Backcountry Boundary

Pocahontas Trail #263

Kennison Mt. (4383 ft.) X

Kennison Mountain Trail #244

55

39

Fork Mountain Trail #236

North Fork

Cherry River

Summit Lake Campground

Rocky Knob (4430 ft.) X

To Richwood

N

Cranberry Area Profile

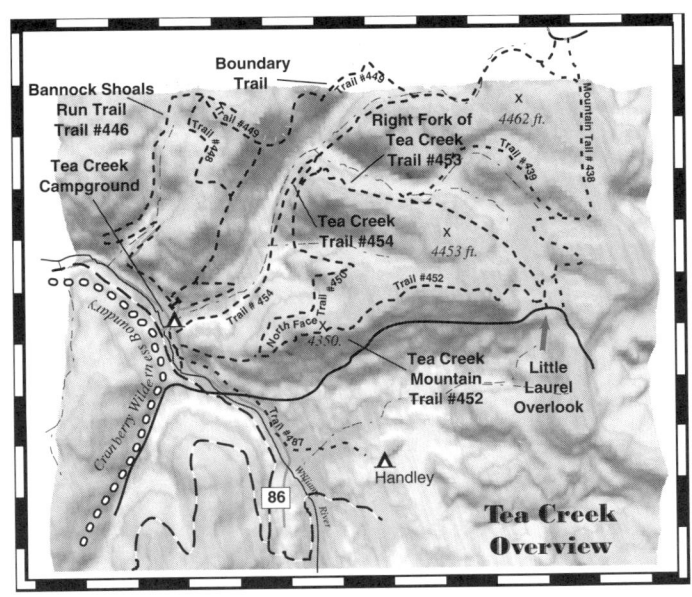

Tea Creek Overview

Boundary Trail

Bannock Shoals Run Trail Trail #446

Tea Creek Campground

Right Fork of Tea Creek Trail #453

Tea Creek Trail #454

Trail #448

Trail #449

x 4462 ft.

Mountain Trail #438

Trail #459

x 4453 ft.

Trail #450

Trail #452

North Face x 4350

Tea Creek Mountain Trail #452

Little Laurel Overlook

Cranberry Wilderness Boundary

Trail #454

Trail #67

Williams River

86

Handley

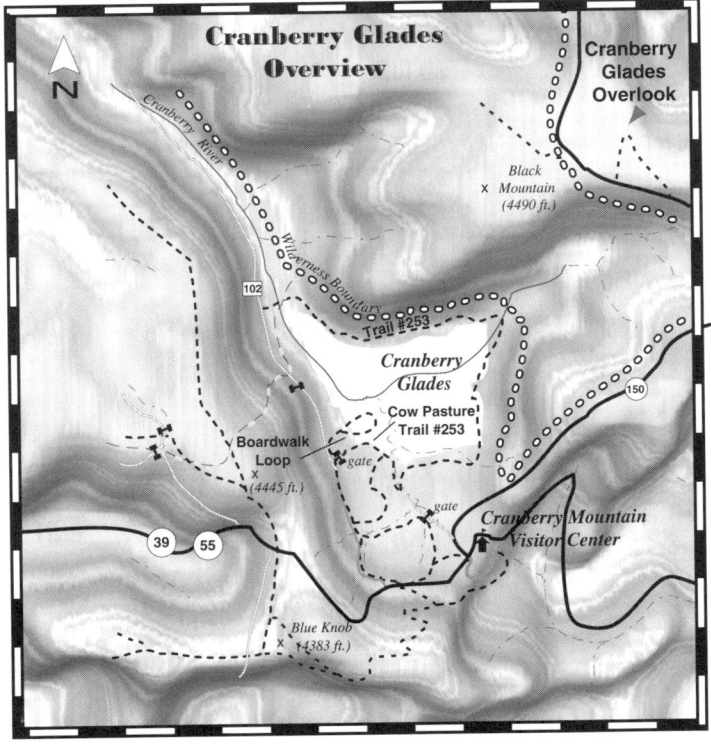

Cranberry Glades Overview

N

Cranberry River

Cranberry Glades Overlook

x Black Mountain (4490 ft.)

102

Wilderness Boundary

Trail #253

Cranberry Glades

150

Boardwalk Loop x (4445 ft.)

Cow Pasture Trail #253

gate

gate

Cranberry Mountain Visitor Center

39 55

Blue Knob x (4383 ft.)

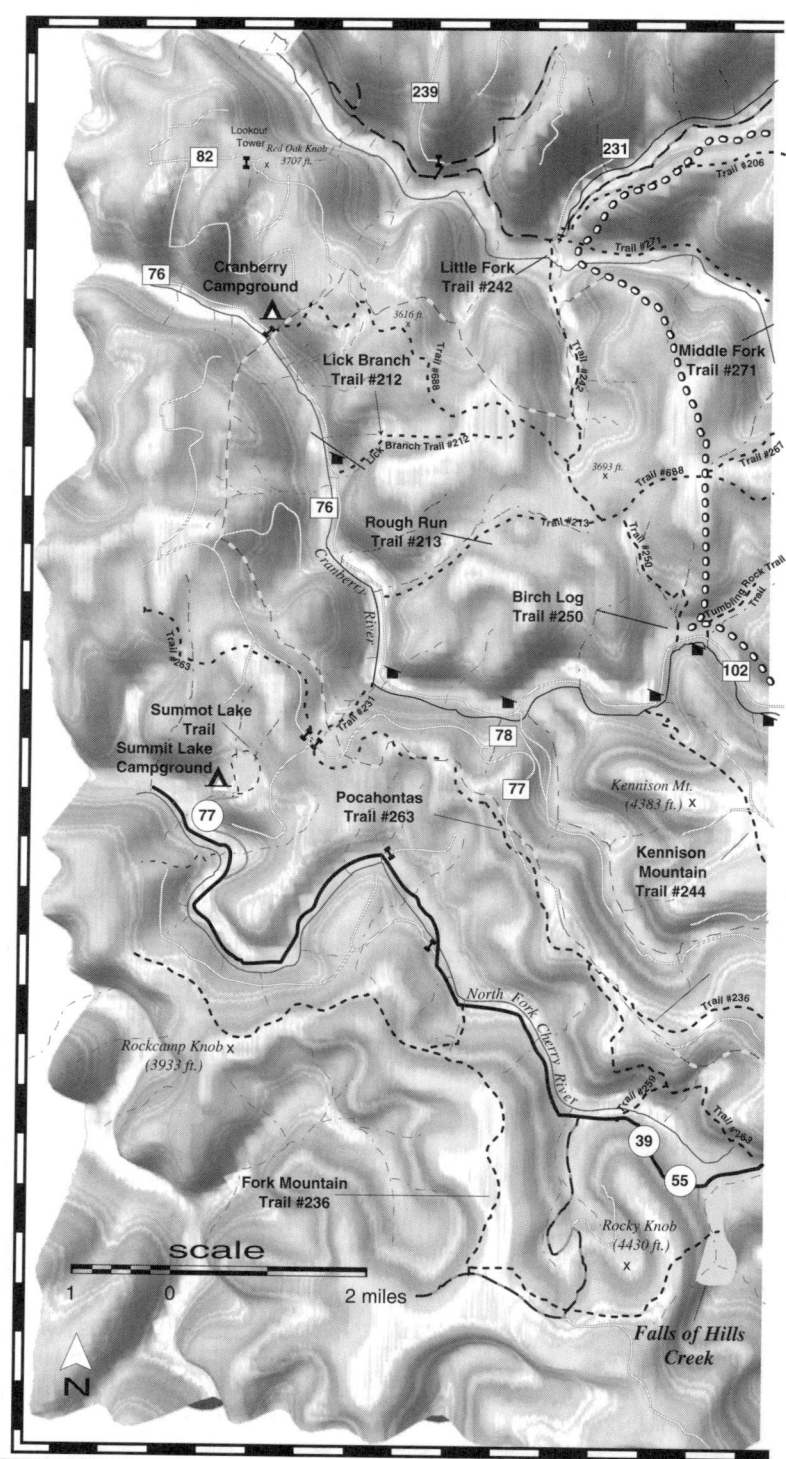

239

231

Trail #206

82

Lookout
Tower
Red Oak Knob
3707 ft.

Trail #271

76

Cranberry
Campground

Little Fork
Trail #242

3616 ft.

Trail #688

Trail #206

Middle Fork
Trail #271

Lick Branch
Trail #212

Lick Branch Trail #212

3693 ft.

Trail #688

Trail #267

76

Rough Run
Trail #213

Trail #213

Trail #252

Tumbling Rock Trail

Cranberry River

Birch Log
Trail #250

Trail #263

Trail #251

78

102

Summot Lake
Trail

Summit Lake
Campground

77

Pocahontas
Trail #263

77

Kennison Mt.
(4383 ft.) X

Kennison
Mountain
Trail #244

North Fork Cherry River

Trail #236

Rockcamp Knob X
(3933 ft.)

Trail #250

Trail #263

39

55

Fork Mountain
Trail #236

Rocky Knob
(4430 ft.)
X

scale

1   0   2 miles

N

Falls of Hills
Creek

78 Greenbrier Trail and Cranberry Wilderness

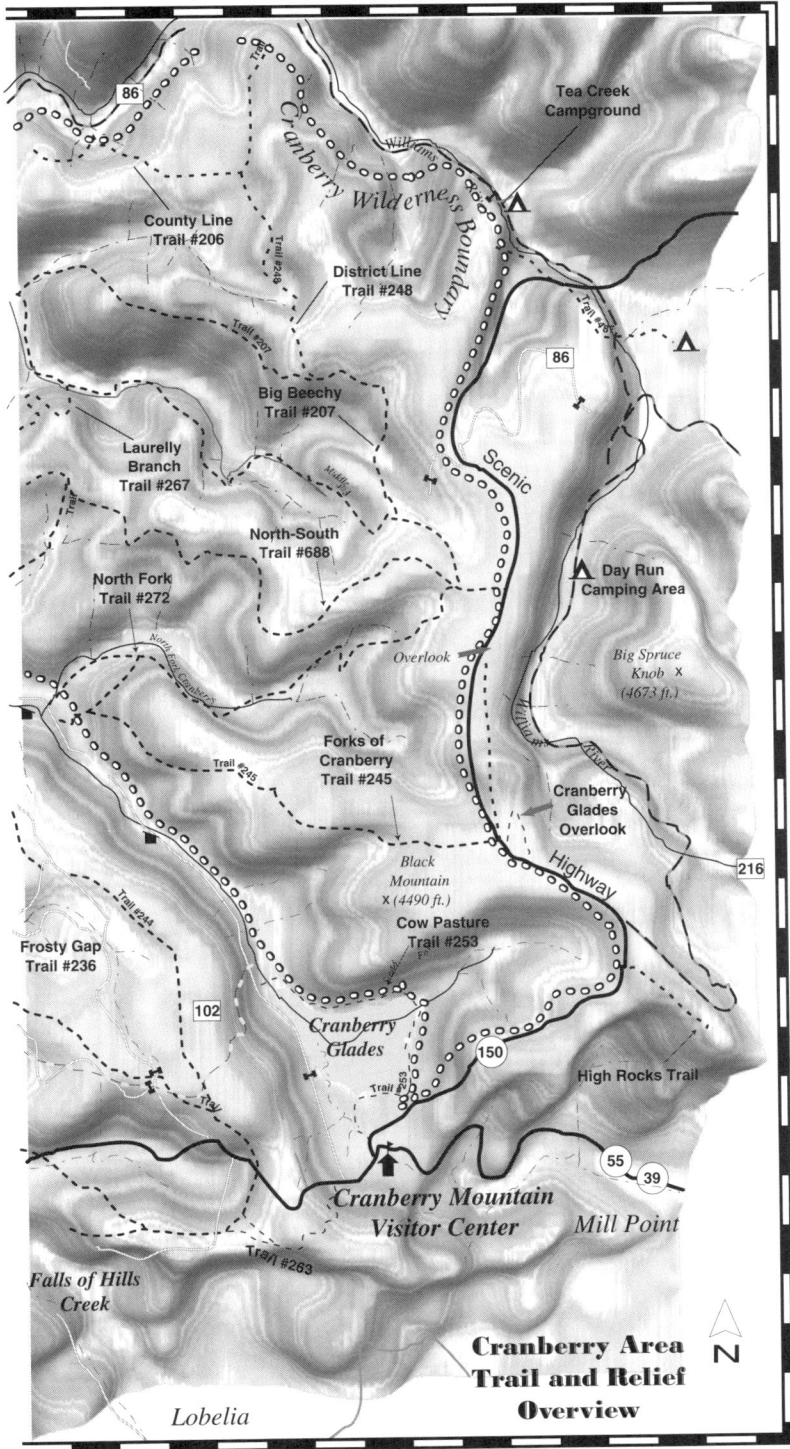

Cranberry Area Trail and Relief Overview

County Line Trail #206

District Line Trail #248

Big Beechy Trail #207

Laurelly Branch Trail #267

North-South Trail #688

North Fork Trail #272

Forks of Cranberry Trail #245

Frosty Gap Trail #236

Cow Pasture Trail #253

Black Mountain X (4490 ft.)

Cranberry Glades

Cranberry Mountain Visitor Center

Falls of Hills Creek

Lobelia

Mill Point

High Rocks Trail

Cranberry Glades Overlook

Big Spruce Knob X (4673 ft.)

Day Run Camping Area

Tea Creek Campground

Cranberry Wilderness Boundary

Wilderness

Scenic

Highway

Overlook

Trail #248

Trail #207

Trail #245

Trail #244

Trail #253

Trail #263

North Fork Cranberry

86

216

102

150

55 39

N

Trail Name	Trail #	Distance (miles)	Type	Difficulty	Mode
Adkins Rockhouse	#228	2	Valley	Moderate	🥾 ⚙
Bannock Shoals Run Tea Creek Camp to Boundary Trail	#446	4	Valley to Ridge	Moderate	🥾 ⚙
Barrenshe	#256	4.5	Ridge	Moderate	🥾 ⚙
Big Beechy	#207	6.5	Ridge	Moderate	🥾
Big Run	#237	1	Valley	Moderate	🥾 ⚙
Birch Log	#250	3	Valley	Moderate	🥾 ⚙
Boundry Trail	#449	6.5	Ridge	Moderate	🥾
County Line	#206	9			🥾 ⚙
Trailhead to District Line Trail		7	Ridge	Moderate	
District Line Trail to 86		2			
Cow Pasture	#253	6	Valley	Easy	🥾 ⚙
Cranberry Ridge	#223	6	Ridge	Moderate	🥾 ⚙
District Line	#248	3	Ridge	Moderate	🥾
Eagle Camp	#259	1	Valley	Easy	🥾 ⚙
Fishermans	#231	1.5	Valley	Easy	🥾 ⚙
Fork Mountain	#236	19			
Rt.39 to Big Run		10			🥾 ⚙
Big Run to Forest Road 223		4.5	Ridge	Difficult	
Forest Road 223 to Falls of Hills		3			
Falls of Hills Creek to Pocahontas Trail		1.5			
Forks of Cranberry	#245	6	Ridge	Moderate	🥾
Frosty Gap	#235	1	Valley	Easy	🥾 ⚙
High Rocks		1.5	Ridge	Easy	🥾 ⚙
Hinkle Branch	#219	1.5	Valley	Easy	🥾 ⚙
Kennison Mountain	#244	10	Ridge	Difficult	🥾 ⚙
Laurelly Branch	#267	3.5	Valley	Moderate	🥾
Lick Branch	#212	2	Valley	Moderate	🥾 ⚙
Little Branch	#242	3.5	Valley	Moderate	🥾

Trail Name	Trail #	Distance (miles)	Type	Difficulty	Mode
Middle Fork	#271	**9**	Valley	Moderate	
Mountain Trail	#438	**4**	Ridge	Moderate	
North Face Trail	#454	**3.7**	Valley-Ridge	Difficult	
North Fork	#272	**7.5**	Valley	Moderate	
North-South	#688	**14**			
Cranberry Campground to Lick Branch		5			
Lick Branch to Birch Log Trail		2	Ridge	Difficult	
Birch Log to Tumbling Rock		2.5			
Tumbling Rock to Highway		4.5			
Pocahontas	#263	**17.5**			
Visitor Center to Rt. 39		5			
Rt. 39 to Forest Road 77		9	Ridge	Difficult	
Forest Road 77 to Forest Road 99		3.5			
Rough Run	#213	**3**	Valley	Moderate	
Summit Lake Trail		**1.8**	Loop	Easy	
Tea Creek Trail	#454	**6.5**	Valley	Very Difficult	
Tea Creek Mountain Trail	#452	**7**	Ridge	Very Difficult	
Tea Creek, Right Fork	#053	**3.5**	Valley	Very Difficult	
Tumbling Rock	#214	**2.5**	Vally	Moderate	

Difficulty ratings on the charts above are intended for hiking. For an idea on how difficult the biking would be for a trail step it up one level of difficulty. Much of the riding in the Cranberry area is very rocky and technically difficult. The easiest rides are on the forest service roads. For example, for the average rider the Tea Creek Trail would be extremely difficult on a bike especially if the trails are wet. If you intend to ride in the area start off on an easier ride to see how it feels and then launch off on a more difficult ride if you need more of a challenge. Climbs up to ridges can be very steep and rocky and the ridges can also be rocky. Remember that not all trails are open to bikes.

Recommended Trails

Cow Pasture Trail- This is an excellent trail that loops around the Cranberry Glades. Trailheads are located near the Visitor Center off Scenic Highway 150 and on Forest Road 102. The trail is relatively flat and passes through forests, open fields and glades. Many parts of the trail are low lying and may have wet, muddy sections.

Kennison Mountain Trail- Trailhead is 2 miles west of the Visitor Center on Rt. 39/55. From the trailhead, this rugged trail gradually ascends Kennison Mountain following the ridge. Near the top the trail passes through a beautiful Spruce forest, well worth the hike. The descent to Cranberry River is short and steep.

Summit Lake Trail- This is a short trail that loops Summit Lake. Trailhead is located at the Summit Lake Camping Area. Trail is relatively flat and passes through hardwood forests.

Fork Mountain Trail- Fork Mountain Trail runs parallel and south of Rt. 39/55. Access to this trail is at several locations along Rt. 39/55. The majority of the trail is on a high ridge where there are few streams for water.

Pocahontas Trail- The eastern trailhead is located at the Cranberry Visitor Center on Rt. 39/55. The western trailhead is located on Forest Road 99 about 0.5 miles past the closed gate.

Forks of Cranberry Trail- The eastern trailhead is located on Scenic Highway 150 approximately 4.5 miles north of Cranberry Visitor Center. Western trailhead is located on Forest Road 102 approximately 6 miles north of Rt. 39/55.

Lick Branch Trail- The western trailhead is located about 2 miles south of Cranberry Campground on Forest Road 76. The eastern trailhead is a connection with the North-South Trail. This short, steep and scenic trail parallels Lick Branch.

Scenic Highway- This road makes a nice bike ride and cross country ski trail in the winter.

Forest Service Roads- Many of the Forest Service Roads are excellent mountain biking routes for beginner and moderate riders.

Additional Information

All of the areas covered in this book are available on detailed United States Geological Survey Maps (USGS Maps). These maps may be purchased at most outdoor retail stores. Below is a list of maps that cover the areas in this book.

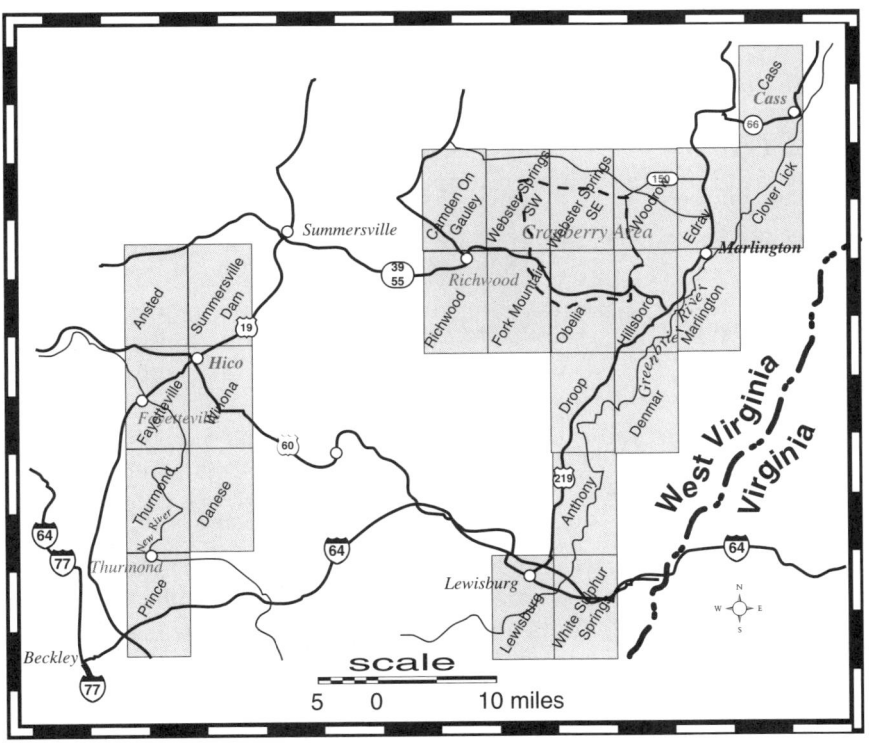

Other Guidebooks

Below is a list of Guidebooks that may be useful if you plan to visit the area.

Hiking The Mountain State The Trails of West Virginia
Author- Allen de Hart.
Distributor- Globe Pequot Press, Old Saybrook, CT 06475

Monongahela National Forest Hiking Guide
Author- Allen de Hart and Bruce Sundquist.
Publisher- West Virginia Highlands Conservancy, PO Box 306, Charleston, WV 25321.

Mountain Biking in West Virginia
Author- Frank Hutchins.
Publisher- Quarrier Press, 118 Capitol Street, Charleston, WV 25301.

New River Gorge: Rock Climbers' Guidebook
Author- Steve Cater.
Publisher- King Coal Propaganda, PO Box 471, Fayetteville, WV 25840.

Slaty Fork Mountain Bike Trail Guide Map
Author- Paul A. Adkins.
Distributors- Elk River Touring Center, Highway 219, Star Route, Slatyfork, WV 26291.

Southeastern WhiteWater
Author- Monte Smith.
Publisher- Pahsimeroi Press, PO Box 190442, Boise, ID 83709.

Wildwater West Virginia
Author- Paul Davidson, Dirk Davidson, Ward Elstor, Charlie Walbridge.
Publisher- Menasha Ridge Press, 3169 Cahaba Heights Road, Birmingham, AL 35259.

Kenny Parker has spent 10 years in the outdoor retail business and over 15 years pursuing his love for outdoor sports.

Equipment needs for hiking and backpacking vary, depending on the needs, wants and energy of the hiker. Choosing sturdy boots and a good pack are early crucial decisions. There is a wide selection in the market today with many high quality choices. Go for a good fit rather than a name or look. You'll appreciate it later while on the trail. Choosing a pack which suits your activities is the best approach to buying one. If day hikes are your thing, don't spend a lot of money on size or gadgets which are not useful. What are you going to put in the pack? Water vessels and water purifier, trail guides, topo maps, books, cameras, binoculars and sunglasses are all things that take up space. And don't forget food! If you have a healthy appetite, buy a bigger pack!

Making a smart boot choice requires more research. All feet are different, so don't base your decision on what your friends are wearing. Try a variety of boots and don't rush it. Wear them around the store or at home before committing to a pair. (Any reputable shop will let you do this to insure you've made the correct decision). For day hiking, a lighter, softer boot is recommended. If you plan on carrying heavy loads for multiple day trips, try a heavier stiffer boot.

If you are ambitious and move from day hikes to multiple day backpacking trips, then more decisions await you. Choose gear such as a tent, sleeping bag and pad, camp stove, cookware and rain gear based on your goals and trips. If you plan on using the equipment several times a year, then don't buy top-end gear. You'll never realize the difference in the extra dollars you paid. But, if you intend to pursue an active outdoor life, expensive gear will pay for itself. It's just like anything else in life, you get what you pay for.

The list of accessories that make hiking and backpacking easier goes on and on. What's important is what *you* think you need or want. There are minimalists and gearhounds. Only you can decide which category you are in. Don't be afraid to ask questions in an outdoor store, most shop employees have been through exactly what you're going through and may offer good advice. Just remember that you're in this for fun! It doesn't have to be some fitness craze or a work-like stress. Enjoy the time spent outdoors. Make the decision process a way to build anticipation for that awesome trip you've spent months planning. And when you return home, and are reminiscing on what a great adventure you had, evaluate your gear choices and plan your next trip. Well, that other tent was 4 ozs. lighter...........

Kaymor #4\1